The Vulnerable Adolescent

Raising Awareness of the Social and Economic Consequences of Adolescent Pregnancy

Noel Holder, AA

Copyright © 2023 by Noel Holder

All rights reserved.

All Scripture references are from

New International Version unless noted otherwise.

DEDICATION

The Vulnerable Adolescent: Raising Awareness of the Social and Economic Consequences of Adolescent Pregnancy is dedicated to all the adolescent girls throughout the world struggling to understand the dilemma in which they find themselves and to those adolescent girls who have developed resilience and made an escape to a prosperous life.

Our adolescents will understand their future roles when the conversation starts with identifying who they are and developing their inner strengths of integrity, honesty, trust, spirituality, and self-worth, thus enabling them to increase their self-esteem and focus.

Rev. Dr. Noel Holder, AA

CONTENTS

Acknowledgments vii
Foreword ix
Preface xv
1. Introduction 1
   1.1 Geographic and Demographic Descriptions 2
   1.2 Definitions of Key Words and Terms Used in This Book 6
   1.3 Reality of Adolescent Pregnancy in Guyana 10
   1.4 Rationale and Advocacy 12
   1.5 Program Development Process 14
   1.6 Adolescent Population Sample 15
   1.7 Motivation for Writing This Book 16
   1.8 Conceptual Framework of This Book 20
   1.9 Important Stakeholders' Involvement in This Book 23
   Summary 25
2. Situational Reality 27
   2.1 Socioeconomic Consequences of Adolescent Pregnancy 29
   2.2 Factors Affecting Adolescent Pregnancy in Guyana 35
   2.3 Preventative Programs Related to Adolescent Pregnancy 44
   2.4 Programs Providing Services 46
   2.5 Biblical Principles Related to Adolescent Pregnancy 47
   Summary 56
3. Raising Awareness of the Social and Economic Consequences of Adolescent Pregnancy 59
   3.1 Approach Instituted 59
   3.2 Convergent Design 61
   3.3 Participants by Category 62
   3.4 Sampling Procedure 62
   3.5 Data Gathering and Analysis Strategies 66

   3.6 Instruments of the Study 73
   3.7 Data Analysis 75
   3.8 Ethical Considerations 76
   Summary 77
4. Results 79
   4.1 Highlighting the Problem at a Glance 79
   4.2 Data Analysis Process 80
   4.3 Themes That Emerged from Responses to Questionnaires .. 80
   4.4 Focus Group Thematic Results 87
   Summary 103
5. Discussion, Conclusions, Implications, and Recommendations . 105
   5.1. Seven Themes or Reflections About Adolescent
       Pregnancy 108
   5.2. Transformational Strategy to Implement CHANGE 119
   5.3 Recommendations 128
Final Thoughts 131
References 135
Appendix A: Questionnaire 149
Appendix B: Focus Group and One-On-One
Interview Questions 155

ACKNOWLEDGMENTS

I extend deep appreciation to my wife, Alexis Holder, and children, Orlando, Nina, Noel (Jr.), Shanice, Kenson, Noelex, and Ketana, who have diligently and unwaveringly sacrificed and journeyed with me throughout the writing of this book. I also wish to thank the following people:

- Drs. Martine Audéoud and Judi Melton of Bakke Graduate University for their invaluable support in various capacities.

- Drs. Bill Payne, Yvonne McKenzie, Kit Danley, and Mary Glenn from Bakke Graduate University. These incredible personalities offered their collective strengths and dynamism, encouragement, and guidance even when I was overwhelmed.

- Dr. Claire Henry from Bakke Graduate University for thoroughly reviewing my manuscript and making recommendations. She is a teacher, mentor, and supervisor.

- I am indeed grateful to the leaders of the following organizations and ministries in Guyana for providing approval and access to clinics and institutions for data collection:
    - The Ministry of Health Regional Health Services, the Ministry of Social Protection, and the Ministry of Education Teenage Mothers' Reintegration Programme.

- The Child Care Agency; the Guyana Congregational Union; Regional Democratic Council Regions 4, 6, 7, and 10; and Women Across Differences.

I thank all of you for your love and support.

FOREWORD

Claire Henry, PhD

Bakke Graduate University

When I first met Dr. Holder as a student, I was impressed with his time management skills: he submitted his assignments on time despite his many responsibilities. At that time, he was a lecturer and the head of the Department of Public Health, Faculty of Health Sciences. He had responsibilities for the following BSc programs: nursing, environmental health, medical rehabilitation, and optometry. He later became the director of the School of Nursing in the College of Medical Sciences, University of Guyana, and a minister of the gospel and a moderator in the Guyana Congregational Union. Each of these roles had its attendant responsibilities.

As his dissertation supervisor, I understood and admired his passion and commitment to completing his research. He now reports this research in his book *The Vulnerable Adolescent: Raising Awareness of the Social and Economic Consequences of Adolescent Pregnancy*. Dr. Holder is a health professional with significant experience in researching, organizing, and monitoring health-care activities in Guyana at the district, regional, and national levels. He has an excellent track record of coordinating several intersectoral programs with a focus on health promotion. He has successfully organized pre- and in-service training for a multidisciplinary group of health-care professionals. This training has fostered community participation to enhance the health status of communities in the 10 administrative regions of Guyana.

Dr. Holder started working in the medical profession four decades ago when he became a nurse. He then advanced to postgraduate certification in midwifery. As a nurse, he spent several years working with children in the pediatric ward. As a midwife, he worked in gynecological and obstetrics wards as well as in maternal and child health centers in addition to engaging in school health activities and home visits. These experiences showed him the importance of prioritizing the health of women and children. It is from these experiences that he acquired his passion for advocating for an improved life for women and girls, who are the foundation of families.

This research examined the social and economic consequences of adolescent pregnancy in the Guyanese context and the need for educational programs that will lead to preventative actions that will benefit the teenage mothers of Guyana. To learn about the consequences and challenges of adolescent pregnancy and what can be done to mitigate the outcomes of adolescent pregnancy, Dr. Holder listened to adolescent parents, the parents of these adolescents, and community members.

Undoubtedly, Dr. Holder's educational and professional experiences as a registered nurse, midwife, and public health professional provided insights and knowledge that undergirded his research, culminating in his receipt of the degree of Doctor of Transformational Leadership from Bakke Graduate University, which is in Texas, USA. His colleagues have described him as a "very experienced person in nursing and training; someone who is reliable, committed, and approachable by students and staff." They referenced his spirituality and leadership, which resulted in his being "held in high esteem by many persons in the community." Hence, in 2018, he was awarded a Golden Arrow of Achievement by the Government of Guyana. This is the second-highest national award.

This qualitative study used focus groups, one-on-one interviews, and questionnaires to analyze the attitudes of people close to adolescents to uncover the relational impact of adolescents' pregnancy and birth on the home, school, and community. The emerging themes include the reality of social norms, reflections about pregnancy, the adolescents' new roles as parents, limited support for the adolescents, the effects of dropping out of school, adolescent counseling, reintegration (the way forward), and adolescents speaking out. The data clearly shows that, when given the opportunity, adolescents desire to do whatever it takes to get their lives back. The principal conclusion is that adolescents' reintegration into school, with the support of society, family, and the men involved, is the adolescents' highest priority. The book concludes with a proposed radio and television program focused on understanding the implications of adolescent pregnancy.

One of Dr. Holder's colleagues described his research as a "living work that could generate other research." She foresees "much work for restorative action coming out of the research." The message of this book will resonate with actors such as parents, educators, social workers, and religious workers who work intentionally to facilitate the growth and development of adolescents.

Colleen King-Cameron, MPsych Student, MA, DipEd

Central Assembly of God

The Vulnerable Adolescent: Raising Awareness of the Social and Economic Consequences of Adolescent Pregnancy is a must read. The author, Dr. Noel Gordon Holder, AA, has more than 40 years of experience as a medical professional and more than a decade as a televangelist. In this book, he examines the central thesis and the social and economic consequences resulting from teenage pregnancy, which is a scourge to the teenager, family, and society. This scourge should not be tolerated. His opening arguments highlight the fact that millions of adolescents become pregnant globally. Guyana is no exception to this reality: there is a significant percentage of adolescent pregnancies in the country. The percentage ranges between 20% and 22% for girls below the age of 19 years. The percentage has remained constant at 1% for girls under 15 years, according to the most recent data from the Guyana Ministry of Health.

Five chapters of this book examine the severe social and economic consequences of adolescent pregnancy along with related factors such as cultural influences, the involvement of male partners, peer pressure, and the psychosocial effects of pregnancy on adolescents. All these consequences and factors promote or influence the decision-making process adolescents experience and the relational impact on the home, school environment, and community.

Based on research evidence, Dr. Holder confirms that the absence of a comprehensive program will result in second pregnancies, and he suggests the need for an increase in educational programs and timely interventions, which can lead to informed decision-making. He also encourages preventative actions that will benefit adolescent mothers in Guyana. Furthermore, Dr. Holder highlights the necessity for a robust support system and services from various stakeholders to create the capacity to fight to save our adolescents from early pregnancy and self-destruction.

Dr. Holder outlines the various approaches that are critical for the transformation of the adolescent. These approaches include the provision of religious education and the importance of biblical commands or models to address issues that will foster positive behavioral changes. The research data clearly shows that adolescents desire to do whatever it takes to regain their lives if given the opportunity.

Each chapter of the book advances the author's central thesis and solidifies the need to provide a change strategy that involves parental roles, the concept of a transformational leadership approach, and a methodology that can be used to provide additional guidance that can transform into preventative actions for adolescents' change process. The chapters point us to the fact that when adequate support is given to adolescents in the form of advice, love, care, provision of relevant information, protection, and psychosocial support, it will prevent discrimination against adolescent mothers who find themselves facing the plight of early childbearing.

This book will help decision makers make informed decisions that will address several issues these mothers face and aid in pregnancy reduction. So please read it, endorse it, and use it to achieve excellent results.

PREFACE

I have always had a passion for adolescents and youths and their vulnerability, misconceptions, and lack of resilience to their misfortunes that arise from uninformed decisions. It is believed that adversity and challenges related to reproductive health issues, mental health issues, stigma, and discrimination of all sorts may stem from identity and that implications are dependent upon the whole human experience, which is essential to an adolescent's ability to become resilient during periods of vulnerability.

Adolescent pregnancy, unfortunately, is indeed a problem that affects many families. This complex problem can have social, economic, and health implications and must be addressed. Therefore, this book, *The Vulnerable Adolescent: Raising Awareness of the Social and Economic Consequences of Adolescent Pregnancy*, intends to highlight the adolescent's misfortunes arising from uninformed decisions. The book especially focuses on the plight of adolescent girls in the Guyanese setting.

In Guyana, adolescents face challenges related to comprehensive sexual and reproductive health, mental health, unwanted pregnancies, repeat pregnancies, and gender-based violence associated with vulnerability, such as victimization, insecurity, and risk at the community and national levels. The focus of this book is on pregnant adolescent girls. These girls are exposed to social and economic conditions that make them vulnerable not by choice but by a home setting that may not have provided sufficient protection because a parent or parents may have turned a blind eye to events that distort the very fabric of the moral and value system necessary for the expected outcome of adolescent life. Notwithstanding my focus on adolescent girls becoming pregnant and on their social and economic setbacks, the challenges of adolescent boys will not be overlooked since boys, as with girls, are exposed to sexual assaults, insults, marginalization, rejection, jail, and murder because of the uninformed choices they make—choices they may make due to peer pressure.

Moreover, suppose an adolescent girl is not adequately prepared to take on motherhood. In that case, questions arise about whether the teenager is actually ready for motherhood or whether motherhood was forced upon her by circumstances. Under the prevailing state of affairs, will the adolescent girl adequately provide a foundation for her child or children? Or, if given a second chance, will the adolescent girl be resilient enough to navigate the changing dynamics?

The time has come for people of every generation—parents, caregivers, community members, teachers, preachers, religious leaders, and educators—to enable adolescent girls to reclaim their identity and develop resilience in the face of the severe challenges that may change their destiny. The girls should improve their relationships. I believe that when the conversation takes on transformational approaches, especially the incarnational leadership approach, leaders will be better able to share their experiences and plights with the adolescent boys and girls, giving them hope that can act as a buffer against the significant life challenges lying ahead.

Focus must be centered on an event or events that will bring out the positive aspect of children within the adolescent age group. As parents, guardians, caregivers, and stakeholders, we must be ready to forgive the teenage child or children under our care for whatever wrong decision they may have made and help them make advisable or informed decisions going forward.

With years of experience as a health-care professional and educator, I am convinced that vulnerability exposes adolescents to events that can be life-changing in negative ways. The future can be bleak if the adolescent or someone else does not identify dangers. I cannot overemphasize the gravity of work done over the decades by the following organizations: the United Nations Population Fund (UNFPA), Pan American Health Organization/World Health Organization (PAHO/WHO), and United Nations Children's Fund (UNICEF).

As a responsible community, let us remember that our children are future leaders; hence, they must be taught humility and simplicity, to think for themselves, and to make decisions based on evidence—not hearsay or emotions.

Thinking back on my adolescent days, I remember being forgiven by God and my parents for my foolish decisions. Since many of us may have had a similar experience, it is highly fitting for us to strive to forgive adolescents whose decisions were scandalous and may have jeopardized their future. Therefore, I encourage my readers to step back and reintroduce the spiritual component to life and to work assiduously in redeveloping or even redesigning that moral fabric and value set necessary for the changing dynamics that are so evident. Moreover, my goal is to develop a program to raise awareness of the scourge of adolescent pregnancy in Guyana while collaborating with those who have begun finding ways to tackle the scourge.

I believe we owe it to adolescents to give them a second chance and a new start in life… Will you join this effort?

1. Introduction

This book, *The Vulnerable Adolescent: Raising Awareness of the Social and Economic Consequences of Adolescent Pregnancy*, was written to highlight one of society's tragedies that has often gone unnoticed. The book aims to make parents aware of the subtle but life-changing events that have occurred and that have partially or nearly destroyed the lives of many of our adolescents, especially girls. My aim is also to help adolescents understand that life has many facets; hence, they must never give up because there is light and hope if they begin to make wise choices. This book can be a reference point for churches, schools, and organizations to reinforce adolescent stability, reintegration life skills, and wise counsel.

There is a lack of research concerning adolescent pregnancy and, particularly, the effects of the social and economic consequences of adolescent pregnancy in Guyana. However, some conventions, reports, and documentation from leading organizations are available. For example, the United Nations Population Fund (UNFPA), Pan American Health Organization/World Health Organization (PAHO/WHO), and United Nations Children's Fund (UNICEF) each discuss the challenges of adolescent pregnancies. This book highlights the socioeconomic, cultural, and educational challenges adolescents face when they become pregnant. Moreover, the goal is to develop a program to raise awareness about adolescent pregnancy in Guyana.

Loaiza and Liang (2013) confirmed that collaboration between the Convention on the Rights of the Child and the

International Conference on Population and Development resulted in the following:

- Child marriage and child pregnancy were addressed and often eliminated. These practices curtail children's healthy development and empowerment.
- Adolescent sexual and reproductive health issues, including unwanted pregnancy, were addressed.
- Unsafe abortions and sexually transmitted infections (STIs), including human immunodeficiency virus/acquired immune deficiency syndrome (HIV/AIDS) resulting from unprotected sexual intercourse and abortion practices, were made integral to the health issues mentioned earlier.
- There is a call for countries and the international community to protect and promote the right of adolescents to access reproductive health education.

1.1 Geographic and Demographic Descriptions

Guyana is a beautiful and hospitable country known as the Land of Many Waters. It is the only English-speaking country in Latin America. Guyana is called Caribbean because of its proximity to Caribbean islands such as Jamaica and Trinidad and Tobago. Guyana is multicultural, multireligious, and multiethnic. It is composed of indigenous populations from Africa, India, China, and Europe, particularly Portugal. Over the decades, the children of interethnic marriages and other nonmarital relationships have resulted in a new ethnic group known as *Mixed*.

Guyana is located northeast of South America and bordered by the Atlantic Ocean, Suriname, Brazil, and Venezuela. It is the third-smallest country in South America after Suriname and Uruguay. Guyana has a landmass of 215,000 square kilometers and is divided into 10 administrative regions. Centrally, the Ministry of Communities has overall administrative oversight, while locally, each area has an administrative office headed by a regional chairperson and regional executive officer. Regional offices of health, education, agriculture, and mining and, where applicable, youth and sports fall under the same regulatory umbrella (Guyana News and Information [GNI], n.d.).

According to the Bureau of Statistics, the Ministry of Public Health (MOPH), and UNICEF (2015), Guyana has a population of 746,955, with 49.8% male and 50.2% female inhabitants; 30% of the population is below the age of 15, while young people aged 15–19 represent approximately 11.3% of the country's inhabitants. Fifty-five percent of adolescents live with both parents, 27% live with their mother, and 4% live with their father; however, 10% do not live with either parent. Further, 36% of the population live in moderate poverty, while 19% live in extreme poverty. Three out of four people in the rural interior region are Amerindians (Indigenous people) and are poor (Bureau of Statistics et al., 2015).

UNICEF (2017) confirmed, through reports, that Guyana's highest adolescent pregnancy rate is found among the Amerindian population. Amerindians reside in four of the

10 administrative regions of Guyana: Region 1 (Barima-Waini), Region 7 (Cuyuni-Mazaruni), Region 8 (Potaro-Siparuni), and Region 9 (Upper Takutu-Upper Essequibo). The remaining 10% live in urban areas. Adolescent pregnancy is present in all 10 administrative regions of Guyana.

Based on statistical data, 301,680 people in Guyana are adolescents—almost two-thirds of the population (see Figures 1 and 2).

Figure 1: *Map of Guyana and Its 10 Administrative Regions*

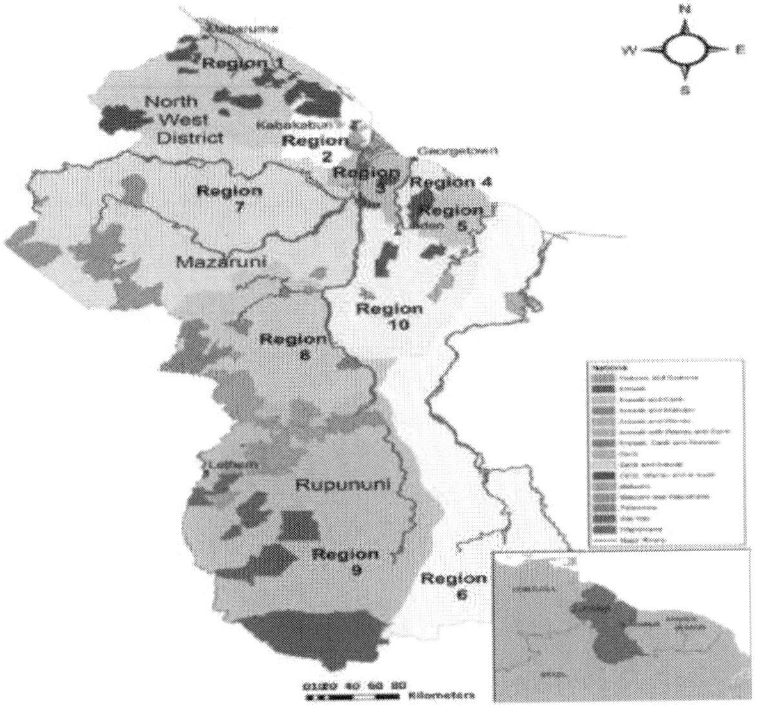

Note. From "The Struggle for Recognition of the Indigenous Voices: Amerindians in Guyanese Politics," by J. Bulkhan, 2013, *Commonwealth Journal of International Affairs, 102*(4), p. 378 (https://doi.org/10.1080/00358533.2013.795009).

The pyramid in Figure 2 shows the population of Guyana by age group and population density. One can conclude that 301,680, or almost two-thirds of Guyana's population, are adolescents.

Figure 2: *Guyana's Population Age Pyramid by Sex and Age Group*

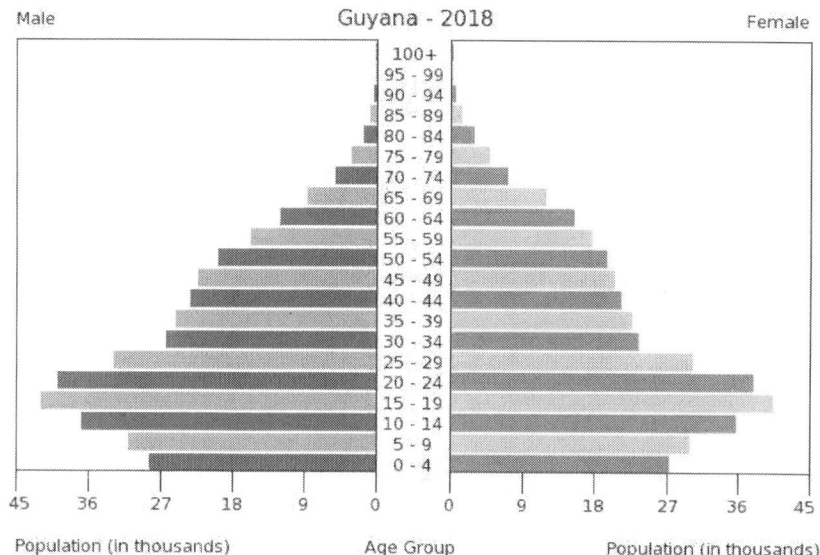

Note. From "Guyana Age Structure," Index Mundi, updated December 7, 2019 (https://www.indexmundi.com/guyana/age_structure.html).

The age structure of a nation's population affects the nation's key socioeconomic issues. The dominant group in Guyana comprises people in the 15–19 age band (11%), followed by the 10–14, 5–9, and 0–4 age bands. Countries with young populations (a high percentage under age 15) must make significant investments in schools.

Globally, adolescent pregnancy is widespread, and Guyana is no exception to this fact: adolescent pregnancy is found in all 10 administrative regions of Guyana. Evidence suggests that 17 million girls under the age of 19 give birth annually, and about 2 million births occur in girls below the age of 15. Most of these births occur in low- and middle-income countries. An estimated 19% of adolescent girls give birth annually (UNICEF, 2018).

1.2 Definitions of Key Words and Terms Used in This Book

This section provides definitions of the critical terms used in this project. The phrases *adolescent pregnancy* and *program development for pregnancy prevention* are a part of this topic that seeks to highlight the many challenges adolescents face during pregnancy and delivery and how pregnancy could jeopardize an adolescent's future.

The term *adolescent pregnancy*, according to UNICEF/WHO, applies when a girl becomes pregnant and is expected to give birth before her 20th birthday. Experts have extensively studied the issue of adolescent pregnancy and its effects are well known, but it is difficult to find a solution to this issue. Experts recognize two sets of problems in adolescent pregnancy: health and medical difficulties dominate in girls younger than 15 years because their bodies may not be mature enough to sustain a normal pregnancy and birth. In girls older than 15, the primary concerns are lack of social and economic readiness for motherhood.

Ganchimeg et al. (2014) defined adolescent pregnancy as a pregnancy in a girl aged 10–19. It is estimated that approximately 11% of births worldwide occur among adolescents aged 15–19 years and that more than 90% of these births occur in low- and middle-income countries. The number of adolescent pregnancies in the window between 10 and 14 years in Guyana is small, but like the global trend, continually rising. However, this 10- to 14-year group is extraordinary since complications related to the physical maturity of the pregnant girl can be severe.

Loaiza and Liang (2013) defined an *adolescent* as "anyone between the ages of 10 and 19." Many internationally comparable statistics and estimates on adolescent pregnancies or births cover only part of this cohort: ages 15 to 19. Little information is available for the segment of the teenage population between the ages of 10 and 14. However, it is this young age group whose needs and vulnerabilities may be greatest, since a child is considered anyone under the age of 18 years.

UNICEF (2017) defined an *adolescent mother* as "a female of school-age (under the age of 18 years) who has delivered a newborn infant and enters into motherhood."

Adolescent parent refers to "either the natural mother or father of [a] newborn infant [who is school age]" (Ministry of Education [MOE], 2018, p. 11).

According to the Guyana Chronicle (2014; citing Daly, 1974), *Amerindians* (or the Indigenous community) belong to the Mongoloid group and "are believed to have crossed from Asia by way of the Bering Strait, an ice bridge joining Asia to the Americas, during the fourth ice age while following migrating prey." These fishers and hunters "brought their skill of making weapons of stone and bone and at some point learned to cultivate the land." Today, Indigenous people use updated tools to continue this ancestral culture within their communities.

Finkelhor (1984) defined *child sexual abuse* as sexual contact with a child. The writer went on to say that child sexual abuse may occur under one of three conditions: when a significant age or maturational difference exists between partners, when one partner is in a position of authority over or in a care-taking relationship with a child, and when the act is carried out against the child through violence or trickery. Finkelhor (1994), 10 years later, added to the body of knowledge by confirming that children are most vulnerable to being sexually abused between the ages of 7 and 12.

The Guyana MOE (2018) defined *access to education* as "a right for all Guyanese." Education is accessible to Guyanese children older than 3 years 9 months and is compulsory up to the age of 14 years (p. 13). That education is a human right is acknowledged in several international conventions as a "multiplier right." School-age pregnant girls and adolescent mothers are denied an opportunity to realize this right: they are excluded from the education process upon detection of their pregnancy (UNICEF, 2009).

Corbett and Fikkert (2014) defined *relational development* as a process of ongoing change that moves all the people involved, both the "helper" and the "helped," close to having the right relationship with God, self, others, and the rest of creation. The authors argued that "development is not done to people or for people but with people" (pp. 104–105).

Schalet et al. (2014) posited that *reproductive (or sexual) health* mirrors and expands upon the definition of health as "a state of complete physical, mental, and social well-being and not merely the absence of reproductive disease or infirmity" (WHO, 1946) and therefore concluded that "reproductive and sexual health is an understanding of adolescence as a life stage defines [*sic*] by physiological, psychological, social and cultural transitions from childhood to adulthood" (p. 3).

Burns (1998) defined *transformational leader* as a postmodern head who can lead an organization and cultural change and bring change to cities through different means. Thus, the function of leadership is to engage, and not merely to activate, followers: its function is to blend needs, aspirations, and goals in a joint enterprise. The process of leadership makes superior citizens of both leaders and followers (p. 461).

For several reasons, the word *caregivers* refers to unpaid family and community members entrusted with children's well-being. The family or community members may include uncles, aunts, grandparents, cousins, church leaders, and so forth.

1.3 Reality of Adolescent Pregnancy in Guyana

Adolescent pregnancy as a percentage of all pregnancies in Guyana remained between 19% and 22% from 1997 to 2016. There are socioeconomic, regional, and ethnic differences in the rates of adolescent pregnancy: hinterland regions have higher rates than coastal regions (105 per 1,000 vs. 69), and rural areas have higher rates than urban areas (81 per 1,000 vs. 55). However, the highest adolescent pregnancy rate in Guyana appears among adolescent Indigenous girls, who have the highest rates among all ethnic groups; girls from the lowest wealth quintile and lowest educational background also have the highest pregnancy rates in Guyana (UNICEF, 2018).

An MOPH (2018) report confirmed that 616 births occurred among adolescents under the age of 15, while 16,086 births occurred among adolescents over the age of 15. Further, the Ministry of Health's annual statistical reports for the period between 2019 and 2021 suggests that 9,350 adolescents aged 15–19 years from 10 administrative regions were pregnant and delivered. This accounts for 21%–23% of all pregnancies and deliveries for the reporting period.

In a news article, Hamilton (2017) reported that Deputy Chief Medical Officer Dr. Karen Gordon-Boyle highlighted intergenerational sex as a problem where young, poor girls engage in sexual activities and relations with older, wealthy men. Gordon-Boyle also stated that there is a problem with values and belief systems: men from Indigenous communities and coastal areas seem not to conform to sexual practices that are acceptable to the laws of Guyana.

As stated, the Indigenous ethnic group resides in four of the 10 administrative regions of Guyana. Moreover, The MOE noted that education is a fundamental right in Guyana. The ministry further stated that it is committed to ensuring that all citizens of Guyana are allowed to realize their full potential irrespective of age, gender, ethnicity, creed, physical or mental disability, or socioeconomic status. However, many teenagers would have missed the opportunity to receive a sound primary education from 426 primary and 426 secondary schools and 322 secondary departments in primary schools across Guyana (Parker, 2006).

Loaiza and Liang (2013) suggested that the "girls most likely to have a live birth before the age of 18 years are those who reside in rural and remote areas, have little or no education, and live in the poorest households" (pp. 20–21). Many adolescents from Indigenous communities have difficulty accessing schools due to their geographic location in hinterland regions. This situation creates the challenge of providing educational facilities and job opportunities. Specifically, there is a paucity of information about the social and economic consequences faced by adolescents who become pregnant and deliver. It is essential to monitor the actions of adolescents and empower them to make informed decisions that will improve their relationships with God and others to foster hope that will result in adolescents making efforts to sustain a desirable future.

1.4 Rationale and Advocacy

This book, *The Vulnerable Adolescent: Raising Awareness of the Social and Economic Consequences of Adolescent Pregnancy*, aims to bring awareness to adolescents across Guyana using relevant information from selected communities within the hinterland and the coastal belts of Guyana to highlight the seriousness of adolescent pregnancy and the complications that may arise from adolescent pregnancy, labor, delivery, and early parenting. Emphasis is given in the book to the socioeconomic and educational issues adolescents face daily. Therefore, there is a need to give adolescents who become pregnant a second chance to positively contribute to their personal development and to society as a whole.

Because of this situation, the gravity of socioeconomic and cultural underpinnings must be used as evidence to develop an educational program to raise awareness of the effects of adolescent pregnancy. Hence, the goal of this book is to help reduce the prevalence of adolescent pregnancy. The program I propose could be used in schools, churches, other religious organizations, public health clinics, youth-friendly centers, and public or private ministries or organizations in Guyana to start the conversation on adolescent pregnancy.

The program I propose is called CHANGE (challenge, holistic, awareness, negotiate, generate interest, and esteem). CHANGE was officially launched under the *Ebenezer Praise Time* weekly television program and served as empowering educational content for all teenagers aged 10–19 years in

Guyana. Since 2010, I have funded, produced, and hosted *Ebenezer Praise Time*, which is aired on National Communications Networks (NCN), Guyana. NCN, Guyana was established in 2004 through the merger of the government radio service, Guyana Broadcasting Corporation, and the government-run television service, GTV. NCN, Guyana is a government-run radio and television station that reaches an audience of 90% of the population of Guyana. Anecdotal evidence gathered through my interaction with viewers in several regions suggests that the *Ebenezer Praise Time* program has extensive coverage and undoubtedly positively impacts the lives of its viewers.

The *Ebenezer Praise Time* program aims to provide holistic knowledge about religious, health, and social concerns. In the second quarter of 2022, with this aim in mind, I launched another program at the University of Guyana, 95.5 FM Radio, which covers a 20-mile radius and began operating on July 19, 2019. The theme of the latter program was focus on the family.

I believe this book will facilitate synergies among organizations and institutions to refocus their program goals to address the issue of adolescent pregnancy in Guyana. The main interest groups, particularly the Government of Guyana, will seek to implement initiatives through the Ministries of Education, Social Protection, and Public Health. The collaborative agencies PAHO and UNICEF support this long-standing fight to reduce adolescent pregnancies to acceptable levels. Moreover, I hope that in some ways, these agencies and organizations will increase their involvement in providing the necessary infrastructure for continuing education for pregnant teens.

1.5 Program Development Process

The *Ebenezer Praise Time* television program will be a springboard for advocacy. Adolescent mothers will be encouraged to complete their primary and secondary education, and other relevant information will be disseminated via the roll-out of this program. Moreover, it is hoped that the exposure and awareness created through the program will stimulate parents and community members to desire to improve their parenting skills.

The program will include positive conversations about self-worth and self-esteem that parents and others can have with adolescents within various communities to influence informed decisions. Also, I hope that the government, through various ministries, will seek to set up additional youth-friendly spaces that will allow thoughtful conversations to continue so as to help teenagers make informed decisions about their sexual behavior. Simultaneously, teenagers facing social and economic challenges can channel their appeals for help through these spaces.

PAHO et al. (2017) identified the trends of adolescent pregnancy rates in the Caribbean and singled out Guyana as having the highest rate of 91.1 per 1,000 girls. This problem of adolescent pregnancy does not lie entirely with adolescent girls: it can be attributed to a system that may have failed them. Moreover, the impact of adolescent pregnancy must be examined using a cross-section of subgroups: parents, families, and community and government agencies.

1.6 Adolescent Population Sample

The studied population consisted of pregnant adolescents with a child 3 years old or younger, a participating male adolescent or adult, and the parents of the adolescent mothers. I selected the participants for the focus groups and interviews through purposive and convenient sampling. The sampling was conducted on three hinterland communities in four regions (Regions 4, 6, 7, and 10; see Table 1).

Table 1

Regions and Populations of the Areas Under Study

Region	Total Population	Return Distance	Type of Population
7	18,375	6 h	Two-thirds Indigenous
4	311,563	30–60 min	All ethnic groups
6	142,839	5 h	Two-thirds East Indian
10	39,106	5 h	Two-thirds African

UNICEF (2018) confirmed that almost 3% of Indigenous mothers had a live birth before the age of 15 years. This rate is 10 times higher than the national average and 3 times higher than that of girls living in the most impoverished families in the country. The Bureau of

Statistics (2018) reported that the population in Region 7, Bartica, which is situated in Cuyuni-Mazaruni, is 18,375. Approximately two-thirds of the population there is Indigenous. Bartica is approximately three hours by land and river from Georgetown, which is in Demerara-Mahaica and has a population of 311,563. East Berbice-Corentyne (Region 6) has a population of 142,839, while Upper Demerara-Berbice (Region 10) has a population of 39,106. These administrative regions can be identified via the map of Guyana (Figure 1) and population pyramid (Figures 2).

1.7 Motivation for Writing This Book

This book is based on investigated and documented factors associated with adolescent pregnancy and the social and economic consequences that confront adolescents during and after delivery. Hence, the purpose of the book is specific to adolescents who are currently pregnant or have delivered, the male participants in this process, and their parents. However, the knowledge acquired can be used by institutions and adolescents seeking to understand the social and economic consequences of pregnancy for adolescent mothers. The hope is that this book will deter all adolescents who are under pressure to engage or contemplating engaging in sexual activities. Moreover, the study findings could allow governmental and nongovernmental agencies (NGOs), churches and other religious bodies, and youth groups to accomplish their mission to reduce adolescent pregnancy.

Loaiza and Liang (2013) noted that if current trends did not decline, 78 million girls would give birth during the next decade, and from 2021 to 2030, the number of adolescent mothers would continue to increase, reaching 86 million by 2030.

1.7.1 Health Implications of Adolescent Pregnancy

The health implications of adolescent pregnancy are real and affect almost every pregnant adolescent in various ways. The expectant immature mother faces multiple conditions, ranging from moderate to severe. These conditions depend on age and maturity, economic status, and the mother's socialization. The situation is critical, so it is necessary for interest groups to focus their attention on these challenges.

Giving birth during adolescence is not only a risk factor for adverse pregnancy outcomes but also hurts the future well-being of the mother and infant. There is an increased incidence of adverse maternal and perinatal outcomes, such as low birth weight, preterm delivery, perinatal death, cephalopelvic disproportion, and maternal death (Ganchimeg et al., 2014).

Concerning pregnancy, Loaiza and Liang (2013) stated that a woman's age is defined as the age at which the first baby is born, and adolescent pregnancy is said to occur when a girl becomes pregnant between the ages of 10 and 19 years. Adolescent girls have a high risk of developing high blood pressure, pregnancy-induced hypertension, and preeclampsia and an increased risk of premature birth.

McCaw-Binns et al. (2012) posited that Jamaica's fertility rate in 2009 was 75 births per 1,000 adolescents aged 15–19 years, which is comparatively high. Consequently, the authors focused on adolescent attitudes toward sex safety, sexual practices, use of abortion, and maternal mortality. Their research confirmed that one in five pregnant Jamaican adolescents had an abortion and that complications from abortions were the leading cause of adolescent maternal deaths between 2004 and 2006. Sixty-seven percent of adolescents reported that their pregnancy was mistimed, and 15% stated that their pregnancy was unwanted.

McCaw-Binns et al. (2012) further provided findings from a matched case study in Jamaica that confirmed that unintended pregnancy rates among 15- to 17-year-old adolescents were very high despite knowledge of contraceptive use and use of contraceptives at first incidence of sexual intercourse. The study showed that a significant proportion of pregnant adolescents (54% vs. 41% for pregnant adolescents vs. adolescents who did not become pregnant) first had sex by age 14. Furthermore, almost half (49%) of pregnant adolescents experienced sexual coercion or violence; therefore, encouraging adolescents to delay their sexual debut and reduce their number of partners may help prevent unintended pregnancy.

1.7.2 Socioeconomic Implications of Adolescent Pregnancy

The ages of 15–19 years represent transition to adulthood. This transition includes both the biological events of puberty and the psychosocial adjustments of maturation. Moreover, the transition is associated with risk-taking behavior and, for young women, increased health risks from pregnancy and childbirth (Senderowitz, 1995). Health and medical issues dominate in girls younger than 15 years as their bodies may not be mature enough to sustain a normal pregnancy and the birthing process. In girls older than 15, the significant concerns are a lack of social and economic readiness for motherhood. The future of adolescent mothers in areas such as adequate schooling and other financial challenges is compromised.

UNICEF (2017) indicated that the Indigenous community's adolescent birth rate in Guyana stood at 148/1,000. This number is double the national average and quite close to the birth rate for the most impoverished population in Guyana, which stands at 150/1,000. Early childbearing, particularly among adolescents, has had adverse educational implications: there have been negative socioeconomic and sociocultural consequences, such as dropping out of school early. Also, concerning child protection, it has been suggested that young girls could become pregnant due to a lack of empowerment and education or when they fall victim to sexual violence. This latter point indicates failure in the protection system, including the immediate protective environment of the family, school, religious institutions, and community (UNICEF, 2017).

In line with their culture, many Indigenous adolescents start childbearing at quite a young age: between 12 and 15 years. Further, UNICEF (2017) reported that 21% of adolescent girls from Indigenous communities had begun childbearing, which is 6% higher than the national average. Similarly, 21.3% of Indigenous girls have had a live birth in the past—a number that is almost double the national average.

Nearly 3% of Indigenous adolescent girls have had a live birth before they reached the age of 15. This rate is 10 times higher than the national average and 3 times higher than that of girls living in the most impoverished families in the country. It is unknown whether early pregnancy is connected to consensual sex, sexual debut, or sexual violence (UNICEF, 2017).

1.8 Conceptual Framework of This Book

First, I explored adolescent pregnancy's social and economic underpinnings and found that adolescent pregnancy's challenges are related to social, economic, physical, and mental or psychological issues. One of the significant challenges is the increase in the school dropout rate of adolescent mothers before the end of the first or second trimester and the adolescents' inability to sustainably support themselves and their unborn children (Azevedo et al., 2012).

Second, Senderowitz (1995) confirmed that health and medical issues dominate in girls younger than 15 years old because their bodies may not be mature enough to sustain a normal pregnancy and give birth. In girls older than 15, the significant concerns are a lack of social and economic readiness for motherhood. Loaiza and Liang (2013) reported that an adolescent is defined as "anyone between the ages of 10 and 19." Most internationally comparable statistics and estimates on adolescent pregnancies or births cover only part of the adolescent cohort: ages 15 to 19. Highly limited information is available for the teenage population that falls between the ages of 10 and 14. However, this population's needs and vulnerabilities may be the greatest.

Therefore, it may be helpful to (a) understand life events, both physical and emotional, that occur between pregnancy and delivery; (b) give the community perspective about the impact of nurturing a child to school age with scant or sometimes no support; and (c) comprehend positive and negative cultural factors that may be helpful or destructive. Hence, all must be willing to participate in societal change.

Third, culture concerning a common law relationship (unmarried and living together as man and wife) has been an acceptable way of life in Guyana. An adolescent girl lacking requisite skills is exposed to parenting and wifely duties (Stabroek News, 2012). However, this culturally acceptable norm seems to give false hope while exposing the adolescent to insecurities and future doom if the living arrangement does not work out, thus adding another layer to her dilemma.

Fourth, the social impact of peer pressure, whether positive or negative, has a bearing on individuals, including adolescent girls, who are seeking recognition (Gulati, 2017). Also linked to the adolescent burden is "the increased risk of psychosocial outcomes, high stress, uncontrollable anger, and serious or disturbing problems with their families, jobs, and finances," which contribute to the dilemma facing the adolescent (Paranjothy et al., 2009). According to Tebb and Brindis (2022), mental health can be both an antecedent and concurrent factor to teenage pregnancy, even though pregnancy itself can contribute to depression. Expectant and parenting teens face the simultaneous challenges of pregnancy and parenting while navigating the developmental tasks of adolescence, thus increasing the risk for mental health problems faced by these teens. In addition, adolescents growing up in stressful communities or home situations where their parents experienced depression further places the adolescents and their children at a high risk of repeated patterns over time.

Hence, the biblical factor comes into play when a girl adheres to religious instructions and understands that the sanctity of marriage adds value to the adolescent relationship within the family structure (Thomas, 2015). Moreover, abstinence is a crucial factor in delaying sexual encounters and adolescent pregnancies and an idea that needs to be emphasized in communities. The Apostle Paul wrote, "Don't let anyone look down on you because you are young, but set an example for the believers in speech, conduct, love, faith, and purity" (1 Timothy 4:12).

1.9 Important Stakeholders' Involvement in This Book

I have sought to establish partnerships with stakeholders who play an integral role in the life of adolescents in Guyana and to add to the body of knowledge of the stakeholders' institutional experiences with adolescent advocacy groups. The stakeholders include the Guyanese Ministries of Public Health, Education, Social Protection, and Social Cohesion as well as the Guyana Council of Churches and the Guyana Congregational Union. I think all government institutions and places of worship are likely to benefit from this book.

The MOE must be considered an essential stakeholder in this project because it has infrastructure already set up through its Life Skills Based Health Education: Health and Family Life Education program (MOE, 2011). One of the primary objectives of this program is to empower girls in schools to avoid pregnancy until they reach physical and emotional maturity and to help young people prevent risks and hardships and positively influence them in making decisions that affect their lives.

1. The MOPH provides youth-friendly spaces for adolescents to have a voice. Health centers offer prenatal adolescent care, reproductive health services, and HIV/AIDS counseling.

2. The MOE is responsible for educational development from nursery to the tertiary level and has a Health and Family Life Education program that addresses sexuality and HIV/AIDS. The ministry also has a policy of

reregistering adolescent mothers into the school system.

3. The Ministry of Social Protection (MOSP) provides social assistance (finance and accommodation) support to single parents and children. The ministry also investigates incest and rape perpetrated against adolescents. Furthermore, the ministry provides a home for delinquent adolescent rehabilitation and subsequent reintegration into society.

4. The Ministry of Social Cohesion develops programs and provides ongoing training to adolescents at the community level (schools, organizations, and clubs).

5. The Guyana Council of Churches, Guyana Congregational Union, and leaders of denominations come together under the council as an umbrella organization to address spiritual matters of common interest to their congregants and the community.

Further, adolescents aged 10–19 years and attending primary, secondary, and tertiary institutions; churches; and other religious organizations and other youth associations are stakeholders and beneficiaries of the current project. Finally, several other stakeholders did not take part in the study but are interested in the well-being of adolescents. To ensure the sustainability of the project, I will partner with the following organizations: UNFPA, PAHO, and UNICEF.

I believe that everyone, irrespective of gender, political persuasion, ethnicity, or situation, must be afforded an equal opportunity to maximize their potential and gifts. Viewing people from different lenses, particularly the lenses of love and appreciation and of a second chance, is integral to the success of transformational processes.

Summary

Adolescent pregnancy is a global scourge, and no government should tolerate it. The government of Guyana, through the Ministry of Health, should address the high rates of adolescent pregnancies in the 10 administrative regions of Guyana. In my geographic description, I have used the population pyramid and adolescent populations and identified administrative regions to confirm the group affected. The factors that can contribute to adolescent pregnancies are overwhelming. The implications of adolescent pregnancy include that once a girl becomes pregnant, she is doomed by the socioeconomic implications of pregnancy and delivery, the absence of a participating male partner, an unsupportive mother, and the community. All these implications contribute to the adolescent's dilemma. The creation of a conceptual framework is integral to making necessary transformational changes among adolescents. I have identified stakeholders, their functions, and their relevance to the study. In addition, I have defined the significant terms used throughout the study.

In the next chapter, I discuss the literature I reviewed to address the problem of adolescent pregnancy in Guyana. The subject of the book is addressed under two distinct headings: (a) social and economic consequences and (b) biblical principles explored through their subthemes. Chapter 2 also includes enabling factors, cultural factors, male involvement, peer pressure, psychosocial factors, the sanctity of marriage, obedience and abstinence, youth focus, decisions, and temptations.

2. Situational Reality

There is a great need for educational programs that can lead to preventative actions to benefit adolescent mothers in Guyana. This chapter reviews the sources that sought to identify the many factors that have contributed to the social and economic consequences of adolescent pregnancy. I also discuss relevant themes specific to the challenges adolescents experience.

Adolescent pregnancy and its consequences represent a significant public health concern in many low- and middle-income countries worldwide. Adolescent pregnancy also presents a social dilemma that has a bearing on the adolescent and her family, public health realities, medical interventions, socioeconomic conditions, and society (Chandra-Mouli et al., 2013). The burden of this dilemma has remained and become even more evident for the Guyanese population since 1999. Educators and health-care professionals must unravel the complex and sensitive situations they need to address.

Both men and women who mistreat adolescents face charges, fines, and incarceration. Nevertheless, there are high levels of incest among Amerindians. Children are forced to work, physically abused, and raped, all of which contribute to pregnancies and abortions. Many young pregnant girls drop out of school or are forced to engage in adult roles before they are ready for adulthood.

PAHO et al. (2017) reported that around the world, approximately 16 million girls aged 15–19 years and 2 million girls younger than 15 years become pregnant each year. Their statistics confirmed that Guyana has the second-highest adolescent pregnancy rate in Latin America and the Caribbean (LAC). As a region, LAC has the second-highest adolescent fertility rate in the world. This rate was estimated at 66.5 births per 1,000 girls aged 15–19 years in the period 2010–2015, compared to 46 births per 1,000 girls in the same age group worldwide. Furthermore, one out of every five girls below the age of 19 faces social consequences when she becomes pregnant. It must be highlighted that LAC is the only region with a rising pregnancy trend in adolescents younger than 15 years.

Further, compared to the Guyanese adolescent fertility rate of 90.1 births per 1,000 girls, it is estimated that rates in Guadeloupe are 17.2 births per 1,000 girls, while in the Dominican Republic they are 100.6 per 1,000 girls. Table 2 shows adolescent cumulative fertility rates. The Caribbean and Guyanese rates are highlighted separately to emphasize the critical issue of adolescent pregnancy (PAHO et.al., 2017).

Table 2

Trends in Adolescent Fertility Rates by Subregion and Country (1980–2015)

Country	Rate per 1,000 Girls by Year						
	1980–1985	1985–1990	1990–1995	1995–2000	2000–2005	2005–2010	2010–2015
Latin America and Caribbean	88.2	85.4	82.5	83.5	78.7	70.4	66.5
Caribbean	91.6	87.8	81.8	77.8	68.5	64.7	60.2
Guyana	**114.4**	**94.6**	**99.1**	**94.6**	**100.2**	**94.1**	**90.1**

Note. Adapted from *Accelerating Progress Toward Reducing Adolescent Pregnancy in Latin America and the Caribbean. Report of a Technical Consultation*, by PAHO, UNFPA, & UNICEF, 2017, p. 41.

2.1 Socioeconomic Consequences of Adolescent Pregnancy

According to Azevedo et al. (2012), the socioeconomic consequences of adolescent pregnancy impact the individual's entire childhood: she loses hope and faces diminished educational goals, potential earnings, and spending power. These consequences affect a pregnant adolescent who is still learning about womanhood and who is unaware of the multiple challenges and risks that will accompany her pregnancy, delivery, and parenting.

One of the significant problems facing pregnant adolescents is the unavoidable dropping out of school because of rigid school policies. Generally, girls must withdraw from primary and secondary schools, church, and vocational institutions before the end of their first or second trimester. This absence results in an uncertain future: the adolescent mother might be unable to support herself and her unborn child (Azevedo et al., 2012).

Furthermore, Azevedo et al. (2012) reported that in the household, there are potential long-term effects on a child, the father of the child, the parents of the mother, and the siblings of the pregnant adolescent. These results have particular social relevance in life circumstances, such as poverty, low educational quality, growing up in a single-parent household, being born to a teen mother, or having a sister who became pregnant as an adolescent, which places girls at a heightened risk for social consequences.

Additionally, Azevedo et al. (2012) addressed the complicated issue of whether poor outcomes for adolescent mothers seen later in life are a continuation of a low economic trajectory. Whether early motherhood is the cause of social and economic crises suggests some action needs to be considered to alleviate these critical issues. The authors further emphasized that most adolescents have undoubtedly modeled their life after older adults who conform to the broad cultural and historical pattern of early sexual activity and out-of-wedlock pregnancies. These elements currently occur in rural and urban communities in the Guyanese setting.

Azevedo et al. (2012) further affirmed that other factors contribute to teen pregnancies. These factors include a lack of proper integration into family, church, and school structures; dependence on the peer group for moral guidelines and information; and being raised in the context of unstable family unions. Moreover, the authors explained how gender discrimination, lack of proper health care and of access to education, the burden of infectious disease, and cultural expectations exacerbate the situation. The authors also noted that these elements further compromise the adolescents' current and future well-being, thus reducing their attention to sensitive issues and the need for well-being.

I emphasize that several factors may contribute to life changes. Corbett and Fikkert (2014), reflecting on the social and economic issues of an adolescent pregnancy, viewed an adolescent pregnancy as an entrapment, especially when the environment is characterized by widespread substance abuse, failing schools, rampant violence, unemployment, teenage pregnancy, and absence of role models (p. 71).

According to Paranjothy et al. (2009), adolescents are exposed to several socioeconomic factors, and these factors become compounded when pregnancy occurs. These factors, among others, include area of residence; parental, social, and economic pressure; low levels of income and education; immigrant status; and a low-paying job. Furthermore, the authors argued that pregnancy and childbirth during adolescent years are associated with an increased risk of poor health and well-being for both the mother and the baby, possibly reflecting the socioeconomic factors that precede early pregnancy and childbirth.

Paranjothy et al. (2009) further noted that the effect of adolescent pregnancy on society perpetuates a widening gap in health and social inequalities. Additionally, for young girls who live in deprived areas, pregnancy can increase their risk of social exclusion and being placed at a socioeconomic disadvantage. Azevedo et al. (2012) contended that public health interventions should aim to identify adolescents who are vulnerable and support those who are pregnant. Also, consideration should be given to conditions leading to poor health and well-being.

Gomes (2012) reported that internal inequalities and problems in education, labor opportunities, access to health services, and poverty are related to high rates of adolescent motherhood. Differences in social strata are linked to the structure of opportunities for youth in rural and urban areas. However, some girls and their families who face limited life prospects may see early pregnancy or marriage as having cultural value or providing a form of economic and social security. Without education or skills that make them employable, pregnant girls are poorly prepared to take on childrearing responsibilities while facing diminished income prospects.

Arceo-Gómez and Campos-Vázquez (2014) provided evidence that teenage childbearing has adverse effects in the Mexican context. The authors reported that teenage childbearing prevents a mother from contributing to her human capital investments and that teenage childbearing may have a deleterious effect on the likelihood of living in a poor household. Furthermore, Torche (2010) explained that teenage childbearing may be a gateway into an intergenerational poverty trap.

As such, the research study has two important policy implications. First, programs aimed at preventing adolescent pregnancies, such as sexual and reproductive education during primary and secondary education as well as access to contraceptives through public health systems, should be expanded. Second, once an adolescent becomes pregnant, the state should provide support through childcare and merit scholarships to prevent her from dropping out of school.

North-Central Trinidad has experienced an excess of unplanned pregnancies. Ali et al. (2009) reported that unplanned pregnancies remain a severe social and demographic problem among the adult and adolescent population. Moreover, unplanned pregnancies are the leading cause of rapid population growth and negatively affect economic, social, and health outcomes. The authors also posited that early childbearing or adolescent pregnancy has great social and financial costs to families and the government.

Yazdkhasti et al. (2015) reported that "unintended pregnancies" are classified as high-risk gestations and occur across society regardless of race or socioeconomic status, and their incidences are highest among poor and low-income women. Each year, thousands of women in developing countries die because of pregnancy-related complications. Unsafe and illegal abortions are among the leading causes of death worldwide. The annual cost of treating a woman for complications arising from dangerous and illegal abortions is considerably high. Overall, evidence suggests that unintended pregnancy is one of the most critical challenges facing the public health system, and unintended pregnancy imposes high financial and social costs on society. Yazdkhasti et al. (2015) noted that "long-term studies confirm that reducing unintended pregnancy incidences would increase labor force participation rates, improve academic achievement, have better economic efficiency, increase the level of health and reduce crime rates among vulnerable groups" (pp. 12–21).

Parsons et al. (2012) reviewed the existing evidence about postnatal depression (PND). Walker et al. (2007) confirmed that PND "is not only public knowledge but also results in a substantial risk to child development" (p. 59). Lund et al. (2010) stated, "Epidemiological studies have found high rates of depression in low- and middle-income countries, particularly [among] women facing socioeconomic difficulties" (p. 59–61). Further, Pearson et al. (2012) reported that 15 studies conducted in four South American countries suggest that prevalence, while extremely variable, is at the high end of the worldwide spectrum. The lowest average prevalence rate was found in Barbados (16%); Guyana had the highest prevalence of PND (50%). Not only is an infant's development at increased risk of adverse effects from the elevated levels of social and economic adversity often encountered in low- and middle-income contexts, but it is also likely to be disrupted by the impact of PND on the quality of caregiving of a mother to her child (WHO, 2009).

Finally, it is evident from the studies cited above that Guyana is not immune to the negative socioeconomic consequences that affect the well-being of adolescent mothers and fathers. However, unless strategic measures are put in place to alleviate hopelessness, inequality, poverty, and dropping out of school, the long-term effects on households and single parents will continue to place girls at high risk.

2.2 Factors Affecting Adolescent Pregnancy in Guyana

The factors that contribute significantly to adolescent pregnancy in Guyana include cultural and relational influences that can have either negative or positive outcomes. A girl's decision to become pregnant, the involvement of the male participant in the pregnancy, and the male participant's lack of support can have long-term effects, including emotional and psychological stress.

2.2.1 Cultural Factors

According to Wikipedia ("History of Guyana," 2023), Guyana's history has contributed to the cultural factors reflected in the acceptance of adolescent pregnancy. During the mid-fourteenth century, the Dutch brought Africans to Guyana as part of the slave trade. The enslaved Africans were either bought or captured from African countries to work on sugar plantations. Sub-Saharan Africa was the largest source of slaves. As Guyana changed hands between empires and as an influx of different ethnicities arrived, various cultures became integrated. Hence, Guyana is complex, and it has become a multicultural country as a result of slavery, colonization, and indentureship.

According to the Constitution of the Cooperative Republic of Guyana Act (1980), the legal age for sexual consent, sexual activities, and marriage is 16 years. The Indo-Guyanese give parental consent for matched marriages of adolescent girls aged above 13 years to an older partner. Additionally, the cultural practice of living together at the parents' home after license marriage, a ceremonial marriage, or under a common law relationship (unmarried and living together as man and wife) is widespread in Guyana. Consent to early marriages or common law living forces an adolescent girl into early adulthood and motherhood, which often contributes to pregnancy and delivery challenges for the adolescent girl.

Mistry et al. (2015) argued that it is inevitable that support groups and multiple stakeholders will build the necessary alliances to develop strategies that will affect an adolescent's well-being so that the adolescent will be in a position to make informed choices. Indigenous knowledge is not only varied and evolving—it also dynamically responds to the changing contexts of situated agents. People are actively engaged in the production, acquisition, and transmission of knowledge that "occurs in cultural, economic, agroecological, and sociopolitical contexts that are products of local and external processes" (Mistry et al., 2015, p. 275). Mistry et al. (2015) further contended that "ethnicity is not easy to identify and isolate. Rather than being something earned by birth, ethnicity is a constructed identity shaped through relations of power and difference" (p. 691).

Child marriage is a human rights violation that limits girls' fundamental entitlement to health, education, equality, nondiscrimination, and the ability to live a life free from violence and exploitation. According to the International Center for Research on Women (ICRW; 2018, p. 1), "a marriage or union in which either or both parties are below the age of 18 prematurely ends childhood for 41,000 girls around the world every day." Girls who marry as children have poor health outcomes, are economically insecure, experience high school dropout rates, and are likely to suffer violence and abuse at the hands of spouses or extended-family members. They are also likely to have restricted physical mobility, limited decision-making ability, and empowerment. On a macro level, "child marriage can also impact outcomes for entire nations where the practice is prevalent" (ICRW, 2018, p. 1).

The legal age for marriage in Guyana is 16 years with parental or high court permission and 18 years without. If a girl under 16 years is pregnant or has a child, permission may be granted for her to marry the child's father regardless of age. The age of consent to any form of sexual activity is 16 years for both sexes (Rose et al., 2016). This study found that sexual activities among unmarried adolescent girls are practiced from as early as 11 years of age, thus exposing them to early pregnancies.

Hindin and Fatusi (2009) pointed out that "the environment in which young people are making decisions related to sexual and reproductive health is rapidly evolving [and] the rates of sexual initiation during young adulthood are rising or remaining unchanged in many developing countries" (p. 58). The authors further highlighted that "early marriage and early marital sexual activity present reproductive health risks for young women, such as the risk of obstetric fistulae" and that "adolescent sexual activity is increasing within or outside of marriage, [and this] can lead to negative reproductive outcomes" (p. 58). Thes outcomes include exposure to HIV, seen in in many countries. Finally, when adolescents engage in unprotected sexual activity, they are further exposed to the risks of unintended pregnancy, unwanted childbearing and abortion, and STIs. What is significant is that coerced or unwanted sex, while being a human rights concern, is associated with these same adverse reproductive health outcomes (Hindin & Fatusi, 2009, p. 58).

PAHO et al. (2017), in reporting on cultural factors that affect adolescent pregnancy, concluded that the elements of individual actions, relational norms, and community norms could lead to poor decision-making. The adolescent is likely to participate in early sexual initiation, whether forced or otherwise, due to inadequate information on sexuality and reproduction and may give in to peer pressure because of insufficient information on the values and expectations of family and peers or due to inadequate support and empowerment about cultural and gender matters about values.

Additionally, PAHO et al. (2017) noted that underlying gendered causes of inequality that contribute to vulnerability to and risk for early pregnancy and to gender drivers are highly relevant in the context of adolescent pregnancy in LAC. These gender drivers produce significant effects at the individual, relational, and community levels and can also be sustained in institutional or systemic responses such as service delivery protocols, legislation, and policy frameworks.

Moreover, PAHO et al. (2017, p. 15 & 18) recommended the following actions that can be applied to the Guyanese setting:

1. Identification of strategic opportunities so as to strengthen responses to adolescent pregnancy

2. Improved partnerships and efficiency in the allocation and use of regional resources to prevent adolescent pregnancy

3. Harmonized approaches aimed at the prevention of pregnancy within the 10- to 14-year and 15- to 19-year age groups

4. Creation of understanding and support to reduce pregnancy before the age of 20; also, engagement in policy-level actions to support multisectoral and comprehensive pregnancy prevention programs among adolescents

5. Individual-, family-, and community-level actions to educate girls and boys about sexuality; building of community support to prevent early pregnancy

6. Provision of increased access to modern contraceptives, particularly long-acting, reversible birth control

2.2.2 Factors Related to the Involvement of Male Participants

Rose et al. (2016) reported that 20% of pregnant adolescents interviewed in Guyana had partners who were at least 8 years older than them, with the largest age gap being up to 32 years. Empirical evidence suggests that adolescent males are permanently absent; take on the role of a visiting, unsupportive father; or make a partial contribution that is grossly inadequate. In other instances, the adolescent male often cannot provide support because he is unemployed (Rose et al., 2016).

Sisson (2012) pointed out that scant data is available on young fathers and their outcomes, although the research that has been done indicates similar results to those of young mothers: "early entry into fatherhood is associated with lower levels of schooling, lower actual occupational income, and fewer hours worked in the labor market" (p. 148). It must be understood that two factors complicate considerations of early fatherhood. First, young men have more varied levels of relationships with their children than young women do. Second, a father can improve his outcome in terms of lifetime earnings by never establishing legal paternity and providing no support for his child or even by not marrying the child's mother, not establishing residence with the child, and providing minimal (or lessened) support (Sisson, 2012).

The findings of this study highlight the issues affecting adolescent mothers during and after pregnancy. These mothers are affected by dropping out of school and by the number of children that may follow the first child. Socioeconomic status and the adolescent's future prospects diminish due to inadequate schooling. Finally, there is significant concern about the lack of data on male partner involvement in adolescent pregnancies in the Guyanese setting.

According to Carlson and McLanahan (2004), the most notable feature of adolescent pregnancies is the low level of education among unmarried fathers and the high prevalence of incarceration. These findings suggest that many fathers are limited in finding and retaining well-paying jobs. Further, the fact that many unmarried fathers have had a child with a prior partner indicates these men have great demands on their breadwinning capabilities and must deal with complexities in their family relationships and parental roles.

2.2.3 Factors Related to Peer Pressure

According to Tate and Copas,

> Peer pressure can be viewed as the central mechanism of transmitting group norms and maintaining loyalties among group members. It can be negative or positive, unhelpful or valuable, and may influence teenagers to do things they would not normally do. Peer pressure can take on a life of its own and may not be destroyed. Further, peer pressure is a phenomenon that enhances or frustrates the way of life of those under

the influence [*sic*] because it exists informally among people who share common values, experiences, ego ideals, and hopes. (Tate & Copas, 2010, p. 13)

Moldes et al. (2019) contended that the social environment can affect adolescents during their growth and developmental stages because they communicate with each other. Hence, they become less dependent on their peers and their families, especially in making choices concerning enhancing their moral values. Furthermore, the authors highlighted that "peer pressure could easily affect the self-esteem of students," and similarly, adolescents can adopt "attitudes towards a certain aspect that they encountered or are aware of" (p. 301). Furthermore, Moldes et al. (2019) pointed out that "peer pressure is often seen during … adolescence … because [adolescents] often seek comfort [from] their peers and [seek to do] what their peers [do] without knowing if it is good or bad for them" (p. 300). The authors further noted that "peer pressure is described to have a positive and negative impact on individuals and even without effect on a person because peer pressure is continuous learning."

Anecdotal evidence from observations suggests that although many teenagers in Guyana attend Christian churches, Muslim mosques, Jewish temples, or other religious institutions, they make poor decisions about sexual behavior based on the views of their peers. Moreover, to be part of a group, they engage in premarital sex although they know it is wrong.

2.2.4 Psychosocial Factors Involved in Adolescent Pregnancy

In reviewing psychosocial issues related to adolescent pregnancy, Paranjothy et al. (2009) argued that adolescent mothers who suffered adverse childhood experiences had a higher risk of psychosocial outcomes (high stress, uncontrollable anger, and severe or disturbing problems with their families, jobs, and finances) when compared with mothers who did not have any adverse childhood experiences. It was also observed that babies born to adolescent mothers are at increased risk of maltreatment or harm and that these babies have elevated rates of illness, accidents, and injuries as well as cognitive, behavioral, and emotional complications. The high levels of behavioral problems in children born to adolescent mothers have been attributed mainly to the mothers' mental state rather than to the mothers' young age (Paranjothy et al., 2009).

According to PAHO et al. (2017), adolescent girls with no education or with only primary education are four times more likely to initiate childbearing than girls with secondary or higher education. Adolescent pregnancy profoundly affects girls' life trajectories and hampers their psychosocial development. Lack of education contributes to poor health outcomes for the girls and their offspring and negatively affects the girls' educational and employment opportunities. Children born to adolescent mothers are also at an elevated risk of poverty and poor health outcomes as well as early pregnancy. Despite recent economic growth and social progress on several fronts in LAC, adolescent fertility rates remain unacceptably high, with significant inequities between and within countries.

This study shows that girls from families in low wealth quintiles, with low levels of education, and from Indigenous and Afro-Guyanese descendant communities are disproportionately affected by adolescent pregnancy. Hence, the rising trend in pregnancies in girls younger than 15 years is of significant concern to governments and countries. Phipps-Yonas (1980) reported that "while the typical teenage girl is biologically ready for motherhood, a complex set of social and psychological variables leads those least well-suited for the role into becoming adolescent parents" (p. 1). Therefore, policy prevention programs should be established to protect pregnant adolescents and their unborn children.

This subsection has outlined the dangers and challenges for the adolescent girl who becomes pregnant. Adolescents who become pregnant are at risk of being underprovided for, are exposed to physical as well as psychological fatigue, and may birth a child with behavioral challenges.

2.3 Preventative Programs Related to Adolescent Pregnancy

Sisson (2012) identified a reduction in sexual incidences because of the implementation of a strategy of pregnancy prevention. Hence, an investment in this strategy was timely because the strategy sought to preserve the overall reproductive health of a vulnerable population. Therefore, if this strategy is sustained, it will encourage healthful practices among adolescents globally.

Preventative frameworks attempt to provide a method of thinking about preventing (or, perhaps positively worded, delaying) pregnancy that is both constructive and goal oriented and relevant to the lives of contemporary adolescents. As Sisson (2012) noted, "prevention efforts demand a drastically different paradigm and broaden the options available to all adolescents, [thus] increasing their capacity to make healthy decisions for themselves and simultaneously empowering them in their roles as parents if childbearing is not delayed" (p. 62).

In Guyana, through collaborative efforts with communities, some programs have been established to enable parents, elders, and religious and other leaders to identify the dangers of pregnancy before the age of 18. Consequently, promoting the rights of girls is community owned, so there are standard solutions to discourage and eventually end the practice of early sexual encounters. UNFPA's (2010) primary prevention strategy is geared toward care before and during pregnancy and delivery and after childbirth, thus saving women's and children's lives and preventing disabilities. Preventing unwanted pregnancies can curb recourse to abortion, including unsafe termination, and reduce maternal deaths. Sexual and reproductive health information and services can reduce the prevalence of STIs, including HIV, to which women and girls are especially vulnerable (UNFPA, 2010).

2.4 Programs Providing Services

In Guyana, between 2015 and 2017, the MOPH, through its Adolescent Health Unit and in collaboration with UNFPA, UNICEF, and PAHO (2017), drafted a sexual and reproductive health policy or strategy. This strategy aimed to provide universal access to sexual and reproductive health services, which was already being implemented in 24 health centers, 24 schools, wellness clinics at 15 sites in eight regions, and 26 community parenting support groups in eight regions, thus facilitating improved coverage and community access. Maternal and child health clinics, which monitor all pregnant women and children 0–11 years, operate in more than 180 health centers.

The Youth Entrepreneurial Skills Training program is a platform for out-of-school youth. The MOSP offers public assistance based on needs that fit certain criteria in areas of financial resources, accommodation, and representation in a court of law. First Lady Mrs. Sandra Granger is the patron for the Adolescent Mother Initiative, which was established in 2008 by the Women Across Differences (WAD) organization. This platform and initiative are aimed at reducing second and third pregnancies. However, despite the platform and initiative, adolescents return to the clinic before the first child's second birthday with a second pregnancy (MOPH, 2018).

McLeish and Redshaw (2015, p. 13) reported that there are "a variety of models of volunteer peer support offered to pregnant women and new mothers in England." However, the models differ in the type of support, client, individual or group delivering the service, and duration. Nevertheless, any form of peer support will definitely create a structure for socially meaningful relationships to take place in an atmosphere that seeks to restore hope to the adolescent.

The programs mentioned above are set up to support vulnerable and marginalized mothers and enable them to access services in ways that complement the work of health professionals. Yet maternal and child health services that are adequately staffed and equipped will reduce all aspects of health complications and facilitate safe health outcomes. The program outcomes will help to improve the girls' economic and social well-being and may aid the most marginalized and vulnerable girls in deferring pregnancy.

2.5 Biblical Principles Related to Adolescent Pregnancy

This subsection identifies critical biblical teachings that are relevant to the moral growth and development of adolescents, who are God's children. The elements of biblical commands on sexual purity, religious education, the sanctity of marriage, biblical models, obedience and abstinence, temptations, youth decisions, and youth focus provide a primary platform for the initiative to set up a transformational program titled When Guyana Smiles, which is based on my findings, using my national television program *Ebenezer Praise Time*. My goal was to develop a program to raise awareness of the consequences of adolescent pregnancy. Information dissemination could be done through radio and television, thus reaching 90% of the Guyanese population, and through workshops and seminars in schools, churches, and youth organizations. The program *Ebenezer Praise Time* seeks to bring about a new way of thinking for the adolescent through the transformational process of CHANGE (challenge, holistic, awareness, negotiate, generate interest, and esteem) under the nonprofit organization When Guyana Smiles.

I believe that several related areas can support a holistic approach to making changes. Such a holistic approach will inspire self-conviction and informed decision-making that will provide hope in what the interest groups perceive as a hopeless situation. Haglund and Fehring (2010) pointed out that "adolescents who held religious sexual attitudes were 27–54% less likely to have had sex and had significantly fewer sexual partners than peers" (p. 1). However, in many churches in Guyana, I have seen adolescent pregnancies among attendees. Therefore, the church needs to play an active and holistic role in the development of adolescent congregants.

2.5.1 Biblical Commands on Sexual Purity

The Apostle Paul affirms, "Marriage should be honored by all, and the marriage bed kept pure, for God will judge the adulterer and all the sexually immoral" (Hebrews 13:4). Therefore, sex outside of marriage is considered fornication, which is a sin by biblical standards. Adolescent pregnancy occurs when a girl becomes pregnant and is expected to give birth before her 20th birthday. The issue of adolescent pregnancy has been extensively studied by experts, and its effects are well known; however, its solution is difficult to find. Experts recognize two sets of problems. In girls younger than 15 years, health and medical problems dominate, as their bodies may not be sufficiently mature to sustain a normal pregnancy and give birth. In girls older than 15, the major concerns tend to be lack of social and economic readiness for motherhood.

Abstinence is a crucial factor in the delay of sexual encounters and adolescent pregnancies and is an idea that needs to be emphasized in all parts of the church. The Apostle Paul wrote, "Don't let anyone look down on you because you are young, but set an example for the believers in speech, in conduct, in love, in faith, and in purity" (1 Timothy 4:12). He also said, "Do not rebuke an older man harshly, but exhort him as if he were your father. Treat younger men as brothers, older women as mothers, and younger women as sisters, with absolute purity" (1 Timothy 5:1–2). The celebration of marriage at the right age will benefit adolescents and society. Adolescents are cautioned to be watchful while maintaining the biblical way of life. Goodman and Dollahite (2006) addressed the subject of marriage by noting that "couples who perceived God to be involved in their marriage correlated with specific beliefs and practices" (p. 141).

One can assume that the epidemic of adolescent pregnancy in Guyana and around the globe is a result of a poor acceptance of biblical principles in addition to social neglect. In Guyana, the rise in the number of adolescent pregnancies in the midst of the spread of the Gospel through various media and from global congregations in the last few decades seems to contradict the values and moral obligations of the Christian faith. Extensive evidence suggests that adolescent pregnancy does not only occur among nonbelievers—it also occurs within the church. This occurrence raises other questions that need further exploration.

2.5.2 Religious Education

According to Jennings (1999), the former prime minister and president of Guyana, Forbes Burnham, in a speech in 1974, said, "Education is the nation's business." He also declared that "the goal is a system of completely free post-primary education." Burnham's pronouncement came at a time when primary education was free and 51% of the primary schools in the country were denominational and owned by the church. In 1976, all schools owned by the church or otherwise privately owned were taken over by the government. This move ended religious education and prayers, which were subsequently replaced with moral education.

Piazza (2012) emphasized that the "Bible is rule-based and structured through the dissemination of codified moral laws and divine commands." According to Jeynes (2009, p. 63), the lack of both school prayer and consistent moral instruction in American schools has had devastating consequences both for the American education system and for the nation as a whole. In *A Call for Character Education and*

Prayer in the Schools, Jeynes made a compelling case for restoring moral instruction and nonspecific religious moments to the classroom to restore a much-needed moral grounding in American society in general. Anecdotally, there is a strong case in Guyana for the reinstatement of religious education. It is believed that there is an increase in deviant behaviors in schools. The church needs to offer more than a Bible club: the church should seek to transfer the Christian education values that are relevant and practical and that can change the deplorable situation in which the world now finds itself. I believe that now more than ever, there is a compelling case for the government to restore prayer to the school system through the MOE.

2.5.3 The Sanctity of Marriage

A belief in the sacredness of marriage challenges the community to reflect on marriage and family maturity. Concerns have been raised about how some people view this sacred institution. Marriage happens between two consenting adults or between adolescents who have parental consent. Therefore, it is not a private experiment or a social contract; rather, it is a sacred covenant and a public vow before God based on the love one man has for one woman.

The Apostle Paul gave the way forward concerning marriage:

> Now, for the matters, you wrote about: "It is good for a man not to have sexual relations with a woman." But since sexual immorality is occurring, each man should have sexual relations with his wife and each woman

with her own husband. The husband should fulfill his marital duty to his wife and, likewise, the wife to her husband. The wife does not have authority over her own body but yields it to her husband. In the same way, the husband does not have control over his own body but yields it to his wife. (1 Corinthians 7:1–4)

Furthermore, the couple pledges to stay together and build a family for a lifetime, which is fundamental to the vows taken during the marriage ceremony.

Thomas (2015) suggested that marriage is more than a sacred covenant with another person:

> It is a spiritual discipline designed to help you know God better, trust him more fully, and love him more deeply. What if God's primary intent for your marriage isn't to make you happy… but holy?
>
> Sacred Marriage doesn't just offer techniques to make a marriage more comfortable. It does contain practical tools, but what married Christians most need is help in becoming holier husbands and wives. (Thomas, 2015)

I believe that the adolescent should seek helpful insights from Scripture and church history, time-tested wisdom from Christian classics, and examples from today's Christian marriages. The presence of confident, God-fearing, caring adults in a given community *is* positively related to the spirituality of youths. The "thou shall not" command is a deterrent against an adolescent developing a premarital pregnancy. The Bible says,

> For this, thou shalt not commit adultery, thou shalt not kill, thou shalt not steal, thou shalt not bear false witness, thou shalt not covet; and if there be any other commandments, it is briefly comprehended in this saying. Namely, thou shalt love thy neighbor as thyself. (Romans 13:9)

Understanding the sacredness of marriage will facilitate and equip individuals to increase their love of God as they reflect the character of Jesus. Therefore, there is reason to believe that the sanctity of marriage adds value to the relational context and that adolescent pregnancy out of wedlock is against biblical principles. The Apostle Paul urged young Timothy to "flee the evil desires of youth and pursue righteousness, faith, love, and peace, along with those who call on the Lord out of a pure heart" (2 Timothy 2:22). The message from churches today must reinforce the need for adolescents to avoid all fleshly desires and indulgences and to focus on life in the Spirit.

The Apostle John used the figure of marriage to refer to one's relationship with God: "Let us rejoice and be glad and give him glory! For the wedding of the Lamb has come, and his bride has made herself ready" (Revelation 19:7). In Guyana, as well as in the rest of the world, marriage, which is the element that ends courtship, is short lived since it ends in early separation and divorce. One can assume that marriage is viewed as a last resort or forced experience, which is against all biblical teachings (Ahamad, 2017).

2.5.4 Biblical Models

Biblical models aim to develop a process to facilitate mentoring and counseling for pregnant adolescents and adolescent mothers based on biblical principles. These models will hopefully change the direction of and plot a new course for the adolescent who is part of a nuclear, extended, or single-parent family.

Bakke Graduate University (BGU; 2016) defined incarnational leadership in the following way: "The leader pursues shared experiences, shared plights, shared hopes, in addition to shared knowledge and tasks." This incarnational approach is relevant to the adolescent who has experienced life's woes and needs someone to approach her with an attitude of sharing the joys and trials of life.

The biblical concepts of shalom (Hebrew) and *eirene* (Greek), which refer to peace and wholeness, are needed in the young lives of adolescents to make them productive and of value to society. Biblical transformation comes at a price: those who function as incarnational counselors in a teen's life must exhibit commitment and integrity. Without these elements, those who want to help could become irrelevant and dangerous to an individual's well-being. The incarnational counselor must, in some way, experience or be affected by the things that are affecting those in need. Adolescents need someone to mentor them even before the commencement of puberty so that their adolescent years and young adulthood can be peaceful.

2.5.5 Obedience and Abstinence

Abstinence cannot be overemphasized, and it is imperative to implore the adolescent not to give in to peer pressure to engage in sexual activities. The Apostle Peter addressed the issue of abstinence thus: "Dear friends, I urge you, as foreigners and exiles, to abstain from sinful desires, which wage war against your soul" (1 Peter 2:11).

2.5.6 Temptation

The Apostle Peter warned that one may give way to temptation:

> Many will follow their depraved conduct and will bring the way of truth into disrepute. ... If this is so, then the Lord knows how to rescue the godly from trials and to hold the unrighteous for punishment on the day of judgment. (1 Peter 2:2, 9)

The Apostle James told believers,

> If any of you lacks wisdom, they should ask God, who gives generously to all without finding fault, and it will be given to you. ... But each person is tempted when they are dragged away by their own evil desire and enticed. (James 1:5, 14)

Finally, the Apostle Paul gave directions to believers:

> I say, walk by the Spirit, and you will not gratify the desires of the flesh. For the flesh desires what is contrary to the Spirit, and the Spirit what is contrary to

the flesh. They are in conflict with each other, so you are not to do whatever you want. (Galatians 5:16–17)

Therefore, adolescents must be taught about elements that may destroy their future.

2.5.7 Youth Decisions and Adolescent Pregnancy

Anecdotally, Christianity is essential to moral, spiritual, and social development not only for adolescents but for the community at large. The community needs to take responsibility for societal changes and improvement or breakdown of values that lead to moral decay. It is my hope that this book will create a platform for adolescent goal setting and behavioral changes to be made a priority.

PAHO (2017) pointed out that while many factors can affect the decisions individuals make during the adolescent phase and even into young adulthood, these decisions can be drastically changed when one considers relational norms, inadequate information on values, and expectations of family and peers. These elements must be analyzed critically to correct them. Furthermore, if adolescents receive no formal teaching on how to make informed decisions, they can face the kinds of setbacks that now confront them.

Summary

The Vulnerable Adolescent examines the socioeconomic and cultural underpinnings that lead to adolescent pregnancy. The literature review in this chapter addressed various aspects of adolescent pregnancy. I have covered the socioeconomic consequences of adolescent pregnancy and the factors concerning adolescent pregnancy in Guyana, such as peer pressure, psychosocial aspects, preventative programs and service providers, the biblical principles of sexual purity and marriage as well as scriptural models, obedience and abstinence, temptation, and youth decisions. I have also discussed the aim to develop an educational program based on gathered data to reduce adolescent pregnancy.

This chapter further covered the literature that provided information highlighting the need for adolescents to avoid peer pressure and instead be enrolled in preventative programs to change their behavior and reduce the psychosocial dilemmas of adolescent pregnancy. In the next chapter, I highlight the method, design, and instruments used to address the problem of adolescent pregnancy.

3. Raising Awareness of the Social and Economic Consequences of Adolescent Pregnancy

Resolute in my quest to explore the social and economic consequences, the cultural underpinnings, and the enabling factors that lead to adolescent pregnancy, I decided to prove that adolescent pregnancy has consequences. I sought to develop a platform that can explain the situation of concern or describe the causal relationships of interest (Creswell & Creswell, 2017). I opted for the mixed-methods approach, which Greene (2007, as cited in Bliss, 2008) described as "multiple ways of seeing and hearing" (p. 20). Creswell and Clark (2017) pointed out that "multiple ways are visible in everyday life" and that mixed methods research provides multiple ways to address a research problem (pp. 1–2). The results of the analysis of the data collected were used to develop an educational program to reduce adolescent pregnancy.

3.1 Approach Instituted

Tashakkori and Teddlie (2003) defined mixed methods as the combination of "qualitative and quantitative approaches in the methodology of a study" (p. 9). A qualitative study was an appropriate approach for gathering the required information concerning the factors associated with adolescent pregnancy. Data were collected using quantitative and qualitative instruments and focus groups and then analyzed to determine whether the two types of data showed similar results from different perspectives (Creswell & Plano, 2017). I used individual interviews, focus group interviews, and questionnaires to gather information on the social and economic consequences of adolescent pregnancy from a selected group of adolescents who were either pregnant or had a child who was 3 years old or younger; the partners and parents of the adolescents were also part of the sample group.

I used structured and semistructured interviews and the focus group methodology to collect data (Gill et al., 2008). The mixed-method approach benefited the study, as the qualitative aspect of the research provided a deep understanding of social phenomena. Moreover, this approach is most appropriate when there is a paucity of information concerning the study phenomenon or when detailed insights are required from an individual participant. A qualitative study is suitable for exploring sensitive topics that participants may not want to discuss among their peers (Gill et al., 2008).

The use of focus groups for collecting data provided an excellent method of obtaining information from participant interactions in a group setting. The use of one-on-one interviews with individuals further enhanced the focus group data, and the questionnaire allowed the participants to select several options when answering each question. The data collection processes added to and complemented the present body of knowledge. The combination of interviews, focus groups, and questionnaires supported a balanced approach to data collection and triangulation for validation. Triangulating data sources means seeking convergence from qualitative and quantitative sources. The original concept of triangulation emerged from mixing different types of data. The results from one method can help develop or inform another method (Creswell & Creswell, 2017).

3.2 Convergent Design

A convergent design involves collecting and analyzing two independent strands of qualitative and quantitative data in a single phase, merging the results of the two strands, and then looking for convergence, divergence, contradictions, or relationships between the two strands. The intention for a convergent design is for mixed-methods evaluation to adhere to fundamental principles (Creswell & Plano, 2018; Hall & Howard, 2008).

Alternatively, one approach could be nested within another approach to provide insight into different levels or units of analysis. The approaches usually have equal importance for addressing the study's research questions. The researcher analyzes two data sets separately and independently from each other using quantitative and qualitative analytic procedures (Creswell & Plano, 2017).

The convergent design could serve a significant, transformative purpose to promote change and advocate for marginalized groups, such as women, ethnic or racial minorities, people with disabilities, and those who are experiencing poverty (Greene et al., 1989; Tashakkori &

Teddlie, 2003). This study used the collected data to generate statistical reporting in the present context. Therefore, I focused on the multiple data sources that would enhance triangulation.

3.3 Participants by Category

The participants in the study were selected from three main categories and recruited from rural, urban, and hinterland areas of Guyana, namely Regions 4, 6, 7, and 10. The demographics of the study were as follows: 127 adolescent mothers (89% of the total), 15 parents of adolescent mothers (7%), and nine male participants in the pregnancy (4%). Almost all of the mothers who were interviewed had been pregnant as teenagers. The low percentage of participating men and boys was noticeable and may be associated with the social and economic dilemmas of the adolescent mothers.

3.4 Sampling Procedure

The study was concerned with the social and economic consequences of adolescent pregnancy and the level of awareness within selected groups, categorized by age, pregnancy or delivery, role in the life of the pregnant or adolescent mother (male participant in the pregnancy, parents of adolescent mother), type of organization, and region. Adolescents who fit the sample criteria were aged 10–19 years and pregnant or had a child who was below 3 years of age. Participants were drawn from schools, places of worship, public health clinics, the MOE, youth organizations, WAD, and childcare protection organizations for the interviews and focus groups. According to the Bureau of Statistics Guyana (2018) census, there are 170,000 adolescents between the ages of 10 and 19 years in the 10 administrative regions.

Qualitative sampling allows a researcher to invite participants who can provide rich and in-depth insight concerning an investigation. According to Merriam and Tisdell (2016), "nonprobability or purposive sampling is the method of choice for most qualitative research since it is used to solve qualitative problems, such as discovering what occurs, the implications of what occurs, and the relationships linking occurrences" (p. 96). Thus, the most appropriate sampling strategy for this study was nonprobabilistic sampling, and its most common form is called purposive or purposeful sampling.

Merriam and Tisdell further stated,

> Purposeful sampling is based on the assumption that the investigator wants to discover, understand, and gain insight and, therefore, must select a sample from which most is learned… the logic and power of purposeful qualitative sampling derive from the emphasis on the in-depth understanding of specific cases: information-rich cases. Information-rich cases are those from which one can learn a great deal about issues of central importance to the purpose of the inquiry, thus the term purposeful sampling. (Merriam & Tisdell, 2016, p. 96)

They went on to explain that "the situation is analogous to one in which some expert consultants are called in on a complicated medical case who are purposefully selected based on their expertise related to the case" (Merriam & Tisdell, 2016, p. 96). In this study, the criterion-based approach of purposive sampling was used to identify categories of participants from two regions (coastal and hinterland).

This section highlights some of the results from the study. The breakdown of the ethnicities of the participants is as follows: Afro-Guyanese (AF) – 66 (49% of the total), Indo-Guyanese (EI) – 25 (18%), Mixed (M) – 21 (15%), Amerindian (AI) – 18 (13%), and Chinese – 1 (0.7%). Concerning the age of the pregnant mother, the numbers of AF, EI, and M were significant in the 10- to 19-year age group, while AI were significant in the 15- to 19-year age group. The 11- to 14-year age group accounted for adolescents from four ethnic groups, while the 15- to 19-year age group accounted for adolescents from five ethnic groups (see Figure 3 and Table 3).

Figure 3 *Study Participants by Age, Gender, and Ethnicity*

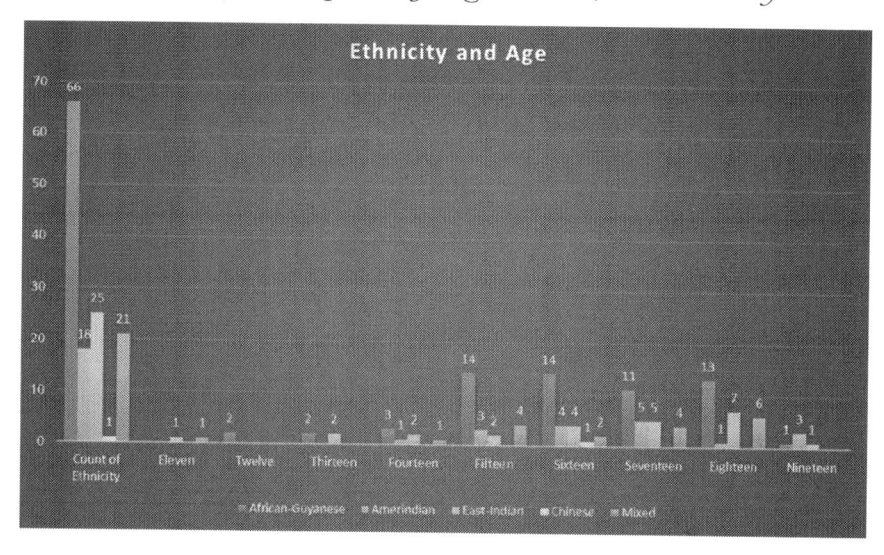

[Bar chart titled "Ethnicity and Age" showing counts of African-Guyanese, Amerindian, East-Indian, Chinese, and Mixed participants across ages eleven through nineteen. Count of Ethnicity totals: African-Guyanese 66, Amerindian 18, East-Indian 25, Chinese 1, Mixed 21.]

Table 3

Study Participants by Age, Gender, and Ethnicity

Variable	Category	n	%
Gender	Male	9	3.6
	Female	225	96.3
Age	11–14	14	5.7
	15–19	109	44.4
	20–24	71	31.4
	25–29	24	9.7
	30–34	7	2.8
	35–39	11	4.4
	40–44	0	0
	45–49	1	0.4
	50–55	1	0.4
Race/Ethnicity	Afro-Guyanese	66	48.8
	Indo-Guyanese	25	18.0
	Amerindians	18	13.0
	Chinese	1	0.7
	Mixed	21	15.0

Table 4 highlights the organizations that provided suitable boardrooms for conducting the focus groups and administering questionnaires. It also shows the number of participants associated with each organization.

Table 4

Type of Organization by Participant Attendance

Organization	Participants	%
Ministry of Public Health	115	49.5
Ministry of Education	35	15.0
Guyana Congregational Union	30	12.6
Women Across Differences	30	12.9
Child Care Protection	7	3.0
No organization	15	6.4

3.5 Data Gathering and Analysis Strategies

Neuman (1994) posited that "data are the empirical evidence or information one gathers carefully according to rules or procedures" (p. 6). Because data collection is integral to the research process, I have ensured that the information gathered was relevant and was acquired through the most appropriate tools.

Analysis in qualitative research can be done using either hand codes, where data is directly input on a typed transcript, or a qualitative data analysis software program such as MAXQDA, ATLAS.ti, NVivo, or SPSS (Creswell & Clark, 2017). The analysis identifies themes and patterns, which allows for theme collaboration and permits triangulation. In this study, data was first directly hand-coded from the typed transcript. Then, a qualitative data analysis software program (ATLAS.ti) was used.

3.5.1 Participant Interviews

I gathered 234 participants: 225 female and nine male participants. These participants were either associated with or attached to five government, nongovernmental, and religious institutions in Berbice, Georgetown, Bartica, and Linden. All invited participants, including those who took part in convenient interviews and made on-the-spot decisions to participate in the study, were contacted using letters. The data were collected via structured interviews, focus groups, and questionnaires. The tools provided immediate and accurate feedback on the social and economic challenges adolescents faced once they became pregnant and delivered.

I used interviews, focus groups, and questionnaires to gather data. I made initial contact with institutions and families to draw potential volunteers and to solicit their consent to participate in the study. Consent forms were used to (a) secure participants' willingness to participate in the study, (b) assure participants that their identities and responses to questions would be protected, and (c) confirm that participants were free to leave if they chose not to continue with the study. Prepared permission letters and email messages were sent to various institutions and individuals (see Appendices B and E). I received permission to conduct the study from institutions and organizations who were responsible for adolescents.

3.5.2 Selecting the Best Institutions

The institutions listed were identified because of their integral roles in child or adolescent development and dissemination of information to adolescents.

1. Guyana Congregational Union—a religious institution that provides spiritual and moral direction to its congregants

2. MOPH—a government institution mandated to provide maternal and child health services across Guyana

3. Ministry of the Presidency, Department of Social Cohesion, Culture, Youth and Sports—a government institution mandated to use sports and culture to ensure that young Guyanese are empowered through interactive programs designed to enhance skills and develop attitudes so that the young can make meaningful contributions to national development.

4. Regional Democratic Council—a government institution focused on community development in the 10 administrative regions of Guyana

5. WAD—an NGO that conducts an empowerment program to equip adolescent mothers with knowledge and skills to enhance their lives

3.5.3 Focus Groups in Action

Once I obtained permission to conduct the study from the selected institutions, I visited them to invite those willing to participate in focus group discussions. The participants were given a consent letter to sign. The ground rules briefly outlined anonymity and Guyana's adolescent pregnancy situation.

Focus group interviews have significant advantages in qualitative research. According to Breen (2007), the critical attributes of focus group methodology is the purpose of pedagogic research to generate ideas to devise recommendations for future change and improvement. The focus group questions were open ended and organized under the following headings: exploration, engagement, and exit (see Appendix B). Each focus group interview session was assigned an acronym based on the organization or institution; for example, MOPH.

3.5.4 Moderating Focus Groups

I moderated the focus group discussions, and assistants with experience in focus group discussions assisted me with note-taking. Recorded notes helped with data comparison upon completion of coding. The focus group interviews were recorded and are described in Table 5.

Table 5

Number of Recorded Focus Group Interviews Conducted between July and September 2019

Institution	No. of Focus Groups	No of Participants
Ministry of Public Health	9	6 × 9 = 54
Ministry of Education	3	6 × 3 = 18
Women Across Differences	1	1 × 10 = 10
Guyana Congregational Union	2	5 × 2 = 10
Child Care Protection	1	1 × 3 = 3
Total	16	98

Note. Interviews lasted 45–60 minutes.

3.5.5 Questionnaires and Interviews for Adolescents and Parents

Researcher-assisted questionnaires contained 17 questions, while face-to-face interviews had 11 questions. These questionnaires were issued to participants based on institution, region, gender, and parents. The number of participants by category and institution is shown in Table 6.

Table 6

Total Responses to Questionnaires by Institution

Institution	Region	Gender F	Gender M	Parents
Ministry of Public Health	4, 6, 7, & 10	35	6	
Ministry of Education	4 & 6	33	–	
Women Across Differences	4	22	–	
Guyana Congregational Union	4	8	3	15
Child Care Protection	4	7	–	
Total		105	9	15

3.5.6 Interview Protocol

The interviews constituted open-ended questions that drew a broad spectrum of information from the participants (feelings, considerations, and decisions). This approach facilitated the divulgence of sensitive information that could not be captured through the quantitative method. All the interviews were audio recorded (Table 7).

Table 7

Participants Interviewed by Location

Location	No. of Participants Audio Recorded
Region 4	4
Region 6	1
Region 7	2
Region 10	2
Total	9

Note. Each interview lasted 15 minutes.

The assumption was that from the interviews, relevant data would be obtained from the participants' expression of their perceptions about adolescent pregnancies. Information about the participants' experiences and journeys as adolescent mothers and concerning societal norms and acceptance or refusal of the pregnancy, including by their partners and parents, were vital for this research project. I hoped that counseling sessions would be available to encourage a change of direction and that adolescents would be motivated to register for any educational programs that would enable them to pursue their future endeavors.

A total of 115 adolescents aged 10–19 years were interviewed in Regions 4 and 6 (Demerara-Mahaica and East Berbice-Corentyne, respectively), where adolescent pregnancy is moderate to high, and 98 adolescents were interviewed in Regions 7 and 10 (Cuyuni-Mazaruni and

Upper Demerara-Berbice, respectively), where adolescent pregnancy is high.

All the instruments, questionnaires, focus groups questions, and one-on-one interview questions of the study were tested before their application. Confidentiality and anonymity were maintained for the focus groups, questionnaires, and interviews. Each participant in the study was allotted a number starting from 001.

3.6 Instruments of the Study

The instruments used in this study were focus groups, face-to-face interviews, and questionnaires. Focus group interviews were selected because they provide an excellent source of information based on participants' interactions in a group setting. Face-to-face interviews accommodate individuals who may be afraid to speak in group settings, and these interviews do not take long to organize. The questionnaires were intended to collect some level of numerical data and open-ended answers that allow several options. The qualitative idea was to develop an in-depth understanding of a few people because the larger the number of people, the less the detail that can typically be obtained from any individual (Creswell & Plano, 2018).

3.6.1 Questionnaire and Modification

The questionnaire used was a teen pregnancy survey created using Survey Monkey, a free website (www.surveymonkey.com). Survey Monkey allows users to create surveys using a question-format template tool to capture the voices and opinions of the people who matter most. The adopted questionnaire template was modified to allow questions to meet the requirements of the study, as shown in Appendix A.

The questionnaire provided both closed- and open-ended questions that highlighted the research topic. Participants took 8–10 min with my assistance to complete the document (see Appendix A). Participants were selected based on the study criteria: adolescents aged 10–19 who were pregnant or had delivered a child who was younger than 3 years old. Men and boys who participated in parenthood and parents of adolescent mothers from Regions 4, 6, 7, and 10 responded to the questionnaires. All the questionnaires were administered and completed at the approved institutions.

3.6.2 Interviews

An invitation for an interview was based on the same criteria as that used for the focus group participants. The same questions from the focus group were administered in the one-to-one interviews. For ease of reference, a convenience sample approach was used to facilitate those adolescents who wanted to make their contributions but preferred to do so outside of a group setting. The interviews were conducted based on the on-the-spot decision of adolescents to participate, and each interview lasted 15 minutes. Audio recordings of the interviews were transcribed to an Excel spreadsheet.

3.7 Data Analysis

According to Sensing (2011), "data analysis is the process of bringing order, structure, and meaning to the complicated mass of qualitative data that the researcher generates during the research process" (p. 194). Qualitative analysis requires creativity: the challenge is to place raw data into logical, meaningful categories and examine the data holistically while finding a way to communicate the interpretation of the data to the public. Hence, one of the critical attributes of focus group analysis is coding, which is an inductive, deductive, and integrative approach.

The qualitative data obtained via the focus groups and interviews (semistructured questions) were audio recorded, transcribed on an Excel spreadsheet, uploaded to the Atlas.ti software, and coded to answer the research questions before analysis. Express Scribe Transcription Software and manual editing were used as support when the transcription program did not identify the speaker's voice. Data from the questionnaires were manually recorded on an Excel spreadsheet from a journal where an assistant had recorded significant additions during the interviews.

The data analysis, which focused on the narratives recorded during the focus group and interview sessions, began with a review of the research problem and research questions as well as an evaluation of all transcribed data from audio recordings and recorded data transcribed from questionnaire sheets to Excel spreadsheets. The multiple sources of data provided a platform for the triangulation and validation of social and economic consequences that can affect adolescents.

3.8 Ethical Considerations

Ethical considerations are a major concern for research, validity, and reliability. Every researcher wants to contribute knowledge to a field that is believable and trustworthy. According to Merriam and Tisdell,

> The question of internal validity—the extent to which research findings are credible—is addressed by using triangulation, checking interpretations with individuals interviewed or observed, staying on site over a period of time, asking peers to comment on emerging findings, and clarifying researcher biases and assumptions. (Merriam & Tisdell, 2016, p. 265)

Based on this understanding, I made great efforts to ensure that research principles were fully applied and aligned with the study's goal.

Previous research indicated that incest and coercion or rape were elements that contributed to adolescent pregnancy in Guyana. In this study, if an adolescent divulged an incident of rape, the interview would be discontinued and the adolescent referred to MOSP, whose mandate it is to investigate such matters, speak with the family, and organize counseling for victims or engage in any other action deemed necessary. No one reported any incident of rape during the interviews.

Parental consent to participate in the interviews was sought for the smaller cohort of adolescents aged 10–16 years. The participating adolescents and their parents signed participant consent forms.

Summary

In this chapter, we have seen that the study used a mixed-methods approach to explore adolescent pregnancy's social and economic consequences in the Guyanese context. The questions asked during data collection focused on the framework of the problem to support the development of answers.

Adolescents aged 10–19, male participants in pregnancy and parenthood, and the parents of adolescent mothers served as the study population. The data were collected via interviews, focus groups, and questionnaires. The results from the data analysis are presented in Chapter 4.

4. Results

This chapter discusses the process involved in analyzing the text transcribed from 16 focus group sessions, nine individual interviews, and responses from the survey. The coded data, comprising selective coding and themes derived from the codes, was used in the analysis process. Also, tables were used to present the results from the narratives in the study and are further described in this chapter.

4.1 Highlighting the Problem at a Glance

Guyana is no exception to the global dilemma of adolescent pregnancy, and adolescent pregnancy occurs in all 10 administrative regions. However, the highest rate of adolescent pregnancy is found among Amerindians (Indigenous communities), a population that resides in four administrative regions of Guyana: Regions 1 (Barima-Waini), 7 (Cuyuni-Mazaruni), 8 (Potaro-Siparuni), and 9 (Upper Takutu-Upper Essequibo). These four regions have a population of only 10,000–26,000 people, whereas the urban population in Region 4 is around 312,000. Moreover, adolescent mothers experience social and economic challenges in various forms, such as rejection and a lack of support from family, the church, the community, or partners during pregnancy and after delivery.

This list of challenges is neither limited to area of residence nor exhaustive—there are also parental, social, and economic pressures; low levels of income and education; immigrant status; low-paying jobs; and challenges to the adolescents' future (Paranjothy et al., 2009). Statistical data revealed that 301,680 people in Guyana, or almost two-thirds of Guyana's population, are adolescents. Guyana has the highest adolescent pregnancy rate in the Caribbean at 91.1 per 1,000 girls (see Figures 1 and 2).

Four specific research questions, in addition to focus groups, face-to-face interviews, and questionnaires, were used to identify factors contributing to adolescents' social and economic experiences during pregnancy at home and at the community level as well as the educational strategies that should be implemented to influence the psychosocial behaviors of adolescents.

4.2 Data Analysis Process

This section describes the process of using instruments in qualitative research. The description includes data collected from the qualitative data analysis software programs that were used, namely Atlas.ti. and Microsoft Excel (Creswell & Clark, 2017). As previously explained, qualitative data obtained via structured interviews were analyzed based on the themes that emerged from participant responses.

4.3 Themes That Emerged from Responses to Questionnaires

I used themes in this section to describe the findings obtained from questionnaires, which answered the research questions. A theme is the main idea or an underlying meaning of responses, which may be stated directly or indirectly: it is an opinion expressed on a subject chosen by a researcher. Themes presented from the thoughts of and conversations with different characters are represented in the responses. Moreover, the participants' experiences in the study provide an idea about the study's theme. Finally, the actions and events taking place in a narrative are consequential in determining the narrative's theme.

4.3.1 Best Age for Reproductive Education

This theme is in response to question Q2: "At what age should adolescents be educated on reproductive health?" Some participants suggested that reproductive education could commence at the age of 10 years. However, most participants felt that the age range should be 14–18 years. This response shows the need to introduce reproductive education early in adolescent development.

4.3.2 Abortion Options

This theme is in response to Q5: "Should the option of abortion be accessible to pregnant adolescents?" This question was answered with a resounding no, with 101 (74.2%) respondents saying that there should be no options for abortion for adolescents and 18 (13.2%) saying there should. Abortion is legal in Guyana, but the lack of adolescents' uptake of abortion suggests adolescents do not use it.

4.3.3 Capping Abortion

This theme is in response to Q6: "Should there be a cap on how many abortions a woman can have?" Responses revealed that 72.2% of the adolescents wanted a cap on the number of abortions, which coincided with the 72.0% figure of the participants who said no to giving pregnant adolescents the option of abortion; moreover, 32.3% of the adolescents carried their pregnancy to term because abortion was never an option for them. Control measures for abortion should be adopted. Finally, the adolescents' priorities were support and advice from a parent, young people–friendly services, and improved sex and relationship counseling.

4.3.4 Mandatory Classes

This theme is in response to Q9: "Should classes be mandated for adolescent mothers?" Participants felt that mandatory classes should be a priority for adolescent mothers, with 108 (79.4%) respondents agreeing with such classes and 9 (6.6%) disagreeing.

4.3.4 Adolescent Pregnancy

This theme is in response to Q10: "Are parents responsible for their children becoming pregnant at a young age?" The respondents' thoughts about parents' responsibility for adolescents becoming pregnant were almost equal for and against: 63 (46.3%) said no, while 60 (44.1%) said yes to the research question. The findings of this study suggest that participants strongly viewed the elements of poverty, absent parents, lack of parental guidance, lack of knowledge, and peer pressure as social factors that contribute to the high rates of adolescent pregnancy in Guyana.

4.3.5 Mother's Age at First Pregnancy

This theme is in response to Q11: "How old were you the first time you became pregnant?" The findings concerning the adolescents' age at first pregnancy were significant and suggest an early sexual debut. The evidence suggested that the average age of the first adolescent pregnancy was 16.2 years and revealed the findings set out in Table 8.

Table 8

Adolescents by Age Group and Pregnancy

Age at First Pregnancy	n	%
Before 16th birthday	64	34.4
11–12 years	6	3.2
13–14 years	10	5.3
15–17 years	71	38.1
18 years	30	16.1
19 years	5	2.6

One participant's views indicated lack of finance as a contributing factor for the high rate of adolescent pregnancies. This lack is linked to poverty, absent parents, or single parents who work. Hence, a lack of guidance to their adolescent daughters and sons is a contributing factor.

Moreover, the adolescents reported peer pressure and physical abuse as elements that contribute to their plight, which should be an issue of concern since the outcomes of these elements are always severe (see Tables 9 and 10).

Table 9

Selected Items From the Questionnaires and the Responses (No or Yes)

Q #	Question	N	%	Y	%
5	Should we offer abortion options to pregnant adolescents?	101	74.2	18	13.2
6	Should there be a cap on how many abortions a woman can have?	21	15.4	98	72.0
9	Should classes be mandated for adolescent mothers?	9	6.6	108	79.4

Table 10

Selected Items from the Questionnaires and the Responses (Multiple Choice, Yes Responses)

Q #	Question	Response (Yes)	%
14	What were your reasons for carrying this pregnancy to term?		
	I could not go through with an abortion.	80	62.9
	I wanted my partner to stay with me.	50	39.3
	I do not approve of abortions.	80	62.9
	I felt that I should take responsibility.	23	18.1
	I knew I had support from my family/partner.	30	23.6

Q #	Question	Response (Yes)	%
16	What would you suggest should be done to reduce the rate of unplanned adolescent pregnancies?		
	Increased support/advice: parents should talk to their teens	53	38.9
	Improved sex and relationship education in schools	39	28.6
	Improved access to contraceptives	17	12.5
	Increased young people–friendly services	25	18.3
17	Guyana has the highest adolescent pregnancy rates in Latin America/the Caribbean. Why do you think this is the case?		
	Poverty	34	25.0
	Absent parents	11	8.0
	Lack of knowledge	20	14.7
	No guidance from parents	39	28.6
	Abuse	24	17.6
	Peer pressure	14	10.2
	Finances	2	1.4

4.3.6 Age of Male Participants in Pregnancy and Parenthood

This theme is in response to Q12: "How old was the person who made you pregnant?" The question about participating men revealed the age of sexual contact with the pregnant adolescent or adolescent mother. The average age of these men was 24; however, the youngest was 16, while the oldest was 55. Table 11 shows that 20 men (15%) were adolescents in the 16–19 age group, 95 (70%) were in the 20–29 age group, 13 (10%) were in the 30–39 age group, one (0.4%) was in the 40–49 age group, and one (0.4%) was in the 50–59 age group (see Table 11).

Table 11

Age Groups of Fathers

Age Group	n	%
16–19	20	14.5
20–29	95	69.5
30–39	13	9.5
40–49	1	0.4
50–55	1	0.4

4.3.7 Pregnancy Status of Adolescents

Concerning the significance of the adolescents' pregnancy and delivery statuses, of those interviewed, 48 (35%) within the 15–18 age group were pregnant at the time of the study. Moreover, 88 (65%) of the adolescents interviewed had already delivered one or more children. Of the adolescents who delivered, 20 (23%) were in the 11–14 age group and 51 (58%) were within the 15–18 age group. Also significant was the number of 15-year-olds who had delivered: 21 (24%). This number was the highest according to the findings.

4.4 Focus Group Thematic Results

I analyzed the transcribed text from audio recordings of the focus groups and interviews with adolescents who had no affiliation with any organization. Codes were used to identify the themes as they support each response from the participants in the focus group session. Codes were based on ATLAS.ti 8 Windows (2019) software.

In the realm of information retrieval systems, the terms "index," "indexing," and "keyword" are often used for what we call "code" or "coding" (ATLAS.ti 8 Windows, 2019, p. 15). The codes serve a variety of purposes from a methodological standpoint. They (a) capture meaning in data, (b) serve as handles to occurrences in the data that cannot be found by simple text-based search techniques, and (c) are used as classification devices at different levels of abstraction to create sets of related information units for comparison. Every participant who consented to be a part of a focus group or interview was given a number from 1 through 10. The letter "A" was assigned to a number when the participant's number appeared twice to highlight a new participant's comments. Identical questions were asked to all groups to assess whether there were any similarities and differences in their responses to the research questions.

Further, three selective codes were assigned to the grouped research questions: bittersweet survival, financial discovery, and futuristic empowerment. Moreover, seven themes were identified:

1. Reflections about pregnancy

2. The reality of social norms
3. Limited support (from parents and participating men)
4. Effects of dropping out of school and type of earnings
5. Adolescent counseling
6. Reintegration
7. Speaking out by the adolescent

I provided extracts of the participants' transcribed texts that may contain Guyana's Creole dialect (nonstandard English) to support the participants' views captured during the focus group sessions.

4.4.1 Reflections on Pregnancy

This theme is in response to Q4: "What are the social circumstances adolescents encounter during pregnancy?" The findings revealed that adolescents faced difficult social situations that arose because they made decisions based on limited knowledge of the consequences that would arise from their pregnancy. Also, the adolescents' dreams regarding family relationships, educational attainment, and employment may have been destroyed. Socioculturally, adolescent pregnancy seems to be both acceptable and resented from the standpoint of "shame"; however, when one examines the aspect of growth and development, many adolescents are not sufficiently developed to physically bear a child. Similarly, adolescents are challenged when it comes to coping with the new role of becoming a parent. Parents, therefore, are urged to have discussions with their children at an early age.

The passing of the Medical Termination of Pregnancy Act of 1995 in Guyana gave selected hospitals and institutions the right to conduct abortions. Moreover, Guyana's abortion law has influenced the sociocultural norm: the act of abortion is no longer hidden. Past evidence suggests that many illegal abortions performed by unlicensed people, including the desperate girls themselves, resulted in the loss of lives and gynecological complications. Anecdotal evidence suggests that many adolescents are either forced or encouraged to end their pregnancies. In this study, 32.3% of the adolescents did not agree to have an abortion even though they were encouraged to do so. The following section contains representative comments from participants related to their general first reactions to pregnancy.

Participants' Reactions

Participant 2: "Oh, Lardie. When I get pregnant, my mother wanted me to throw away the baby. [Giggles.] I tell her, 'You never throw 'way me.' Then I tell she I gon' kiss it. But she cries, she was angry."

Parents seem to have tried in every possible way to express their resentment or separate themselves from the adolescent girl once she becomes pregnant. The adolescents were not afraid to explain what happened to them.

Participant 2a: "Yeah, she was angry, yeah, because uh I just finished a course, I had a lot of umm, subjects on. And I got pregnant so early. So she was angry."

Participant 7: "When I find out, my friends were pregnant. I wish them the best and tel then don't do abortion because that is wrong. I know they are responsible enough to look after their babies."

Participant 2a:

> Well, the advice don't be good. The advice usually would throw away the baby. That's what they advise you. To throw away the baby 'cause it doesn't make sense, they say you're too young and stuff like that. Nevertheless, I never hear anyone say put the baby up for adoption, and I hear one say throw it away.

4.4.2 Reality of Social Norms

This theme is in response to Q5: "What are the behavioral circumstances adolescents experience after delivery?" Many circumstances can effectively influence the decision by an adolescent to become a parent without realizing the gravity of the situation. This dilemma occurs when the adolescent lacks proper education, lives in poverty, and has a family structure that is not protective. The need for the adolescent to accept training as a new mother is revealed from survey findings: 79.4% of adolescents agreed that they needed mandatory classes to understand their roles as new parents. This finding also highlights the fact that adolescents have lost their formative years of life to pregnancy because they lack domestic training and necessary parenting development from their parents.

The ordeal of pregnancy and delivery affected the lives and well-being of adolescents, who reflected on how they felt after they became pregnant and on the community's criticisms of their actions. Adolescents expressed the need for parents to engage in early conversations with their children. Only if they do this will parents realize that they have something to offer. The struggles of the adolescent are evident: they cannot adequately address the repercussions of the decisions they have made. The following comments are representative of the perspective of the adolescent participants regarding their struggles with addressing life decisions.

Participants' Reactions

Participant 3: "I was struggling, wanted to commit suicide, and so, dem didn't treat me good. They vexed with me. I grow up with my sister, she beat me and say I end up with a belly."

Participant 1: "I got here because people report. I was living with my mother and stepfather, but he used to drink nuff rum and only let me eat two times. After my mother find out, she sends me to the hospital to do a test and they reported me because I underage."

Participant 2:

> Well, um, I can't say you can stop them from going on the road and talking to people. Because they still have to go on the road and they still have to talk to people. So, I think that if I did know about this 5-year thing. Where you can have it taken out until you are

ready to have a child. I would have done that because abortion is not an option because of its still a life.

Participant 8:

I never judge anybody because I know people do be in a different situation, and sometimes they might be looking for attention. But when I was pregnant, I was discouraged because I think all my dreams shattered. But I was wrong [pause] at first; I was a little sad because people use to, you know, scorn me an suh.

4.4.3 Limited Support Mechanisms

This theme is in response to Q6: "What are the economic challenges adolescents experience in the community?" Adolescents are still children who still need all the support they can get from everyone. As the saying goes, it takes a village to raise a child. Once the adolescent becomes pregnant, she automatically enters a phase of economic challenges; hence, she needs guidance and support. Everyone should be concerned with the adolescent's growth and spiritual development, educational attainment, and economic status. Furthermore, the adolescent should receive the necessary support from her parents, the child's father, and the church family. That support will enable her to establish a foundation that will lead to a bright future.

The following comments represent participants' perspectives on their lack of emotional and physical support.

Participants' Reactions

Participant 3: "My husband don't want me to work. However, I hope I could get work. I'm not married yet, but soon."

Participant 1: "I think teenagers should have a job. Also, the boyfriend or fiancé, he should have a job too."

Participant 1b: "Some churches, pastor, and people, they motivate you, and they assist you. But some, they talk you down and embarrass you and stuff. I think they should stop with the talk down. Most talk down young ladies when they are pregnant, and it doesn't help."

Participant 5: "My mother put me out, but me child father been like me so bad that he put me with his sister. And she treat me bad; I had to go by my brother. And he treats me bad."

Participant 2: "My father said my child was a mistake, he carries me to the police station, baby father wicked, they want to impregnate you, and then they want to go away. Just drop it in you so and gone."

Participant 2a:

> Some young ladies, when they are pregnant, the boyfriend, at such a young age, at 14, 15, 16, even at 19 or 20. The boyfriend is not there, they don't have a mom to have their back, and they need much support. I had a terrible experience.

Participant 2b: "If the child's father goes away and leaves you, who gonna mind the child? Sufferation."

Participant 7: "Well, if you look around, especially on Bartica, a lot of young girls would be going out, and party, and they get high. And they got no parental control, so they just going wherever they like."

4.4.4 Effects of Dropping Out of School and Type of Earnings

This theme is in response to Q7: "What are the economic challenges adolescents experience at home?" Evidence suggests that there is some level of similarity in the responses of the participants in the study. For example, many of the adolescents (male and female) claimed that they "got caught up" in the sexual debut, which led to their withdrawal from school, rejection, stigmatization, and being left to the mercies of the world. Without education or skills that make them employable, pregnant adolescents are poorly prepared to take on childrearing responsibilities while facing diminished income prospects (Gomes, 2012).

The future of adolescent mothers becomes compromised because of issues such as inadequate schooling and other economic challenges. The following comments are representative of participants' perspectives on the financial challenges of teen pregnancy.

Participants' Reactions

Participant 5: "Some people work when they are pregnant. They do get the work before they are pregnant. I gonna get work just now, is nah nothing hard to do, just books and stuff."

Participant 1a:

> It's tough because sometimes you don't have a job in teenage pregnancy, you don't have a job. Umm, sometimes the boyfriend may not be working, has a part-time job or so. Baby things are costly, then you got to feed you, and when you eat, you eat a lot cause you and the child you're feeding.

Participant 1:

> Getting pregnant when young is very challenging because, umm, you still young, you wanna get fun. But when you pregnant, you can't do the things you used to do before because you have responsibilities, so you have to be more adult-like [laugh]. I would say if you don't want to get pregnant, get contraceptive.

Subtheme: Reproductive Education

Evidence from the study suggests that the timing of reproductive education is paramount to the reduction of adolescent pregnancy. It is also important to note that, where necessary, the introduction of contraceptives (oral pills, IUDs, injectables, or condoms) can effectively facilitate a reduction in the rates of adolescent pregnancies. The study confirmed that adolescents became pregnant as early as age 11. Even though the number of participants was not high, this was a significant finding. However, the participants identified the age group of 14–18 years as a desirable commencement period for reproductive health education.

There were no considerations for reproductive education for an age younger than 14–18 even though the trend of early sex debut was noticeable. This study noted that counseling is a critical approach and a means of empowering adolescents to make the right choice and achieve their full potential. In this investigation, adolescents requested the best guidance that could sustain their needs. Parental responsibility can foster favorable outcomes for children, particularly between the transition ages of 10 and 15.

4.4.5 Adolescent Counseling Needs

This theme is in response to Q8: "What can parents do to allow adolescents to experience a favorable future?" The study's findings identified a critical component of adolescent growth and development: adolescents cannot share their challenges outside of their conversations with their peers; hence, adolescents' appeal for formal and continuous counseling should be implemented as a part of their support mechanism. The following comments represent participants' attitudes in relation to counseling and the desire to be counseled:

Participants' Reactions

Participant 4: "Um, form a group for young people. Get a counselor to counsel them with the aim of trying to avoid you getting pregnant."

Participant 2: "Advise you on the future, you know, don't give up… keep strong…Keep motivating you."

Participant 3: "At least, I would let somebody counsel me, like to tell me. The nurses or the midwife would tell you the next 3 years you would get a better future. So you could prevent yourself from getting pregnant."

Participant 1: "Well, I would say, show them the way, tell them what's wrong from, you know, right. Tell them what is the role because some parents does just sit down and watch you suffer."

Participant 1a: "I think that they should speak to us about not having sex so early."

Participant 2: "They should sit down, advise them, tell them don't do it again. Let the person collect the baby, so we could go back to school and further our education."

Participant 1: "Me mother make her baby early, that's why. She got 16 children; she makes it at 13, early-early."

Participant 1: "I think they should entrust the mother to do the 5 years. I think they should get contraceptives at 16, 17."

Participant 1: "No…yeah! You should go back to school, yeah counsel you, ummm, encourage you, like talk to you personally, like personal. And you could join the clinic, you could join certain parts so you could talk to someone."

4.4.6 Reintegration—the Way Forward

This theme is in response to Q9: "What can the government do to allow adolescents to experience a favorable future?" The National Policy for the Reintegration of Adolescent Mothers into the Formal Education System affirms the right of every Guyanese child to basic quality education as both a constitutional requirement and Guyana's legal obligation as a signatory to several international agreements (MOE, 2018). However, this right is not applied to pregnant school-age adolescents or to adolescent mothers who may have missed school because of pregnancy. Therefore, the National Policy for the Reintegration of Adolescent Mothers into the Formal Education System gives legal rights to the school system in Guyana to reregister pregnant adolescents and adolescent mothers into the formal school system or into other skills-based institutions to complete their education.

This study identified a need for the reintegration of adolescents into the school system or skills-based institutions if the adolescents are to have a favorable future. While the decision of the adolescent to become pregnant may not be justified, her future is essential to nation building as well as to her personal growth and development, including to making academic progress. Accordingly, adolescents identified ways they can engage for their reintegration and the protection of their offspring.

The following comments are representative of participants' feedback about the support they received from the government and the participants' suggestions about how they can be helped in other areas.

Participants' Reactions

Participant 3: "Well, the government is doing a good job. Since I get pregnant at an early age, they are preventing me from getting pregnant again, preventing me from getting AIDS and nuff thing."

Participant 3b:

> I think if they get pregnant so early, they should um, give them some kind of support like um help them some baby things, that would be a big help. Baby things, and probably when they come to the clinic, offer them some lunch or something. Give them some stipend every month if it's possible if they can afford it. That would be an excellent help for teenagers and stuff.

Participant 1a:

> Well, for me, I still use to go to school when I was pregnant. Moreover, I use to feel very uncomfortable in class, and everyone changing their behavior and way. And the moment the belly raise, some is talking about yuh, and this is to make you feel uncomfortable. It used to be like, like you don't want to go, but you willing to go. So, I think they should open a school or classes like just only for pregnant women.

Participant 3:

> I agree that they should open classes for pregnant women. Right, because sometimes young people who get pregnant are feeling like duh is the end of the

world. Furthermore, yuh guh sit down and mind a baby for the rest of life. However, if they open a facility that could encourage them, teach them to go on further with their studies, they wouldn't have to get pregnant. She got pregnant, and she doesn't finish school; yuh could finish, yuh could get pregnant and having a child and be successful.

Participant 2:

Well, I think they should do a-a program for pregnant mothers, like, you seh the thing with the 16-year-olds right, like, they in finish school yet, so is like, just about going and write CXC, they should continue the program but for a class with pregnant women alone.

Participant 3: "I want to go back to school and further my studies. So, when I meet out of here, I don't have to depend on nobody I could get a job."

Participant 1a:

I think the government doing something good because I getting the proper bed to sleep on, meals, and I do not have to worry about Pampers and so. They gon' send me back to school so I could get an education to back and look after my child. They are protecting us from getting sick and getting licks from our parents and getting homes and not having us on the streets.

4.4.7 Adolescents Speaking Out

This theme is in response to Q11: "What final words do you have on adolescent pregnancy?" In the study, the focus groups and interviews provided a platform that was adolescent friendly. As a result, adolescents were able to express and identify their social and economic challenges.

It is interesting how adolescents were able to manipulate their parents and guardians by withholding credible information to save themselves from embarrassment. The following comments represent participants' untruthful responses to parents and the participants' regrets about becoming pregnant:

Participants' Reactions

Participant 3:

> If you do watch at it, most of, most of the teenage pregnancy around here is like rape, or abuse is not really like consensual sex, is not, most people will say, yes is consensual sex, because they are ashamed, nobody is not gonna come out and say, "I was abused by so and so person." So other than frowning on the teenage mothers, I think they should get to the bottom of it, sit down and talk to dem, some teenage mothers just sit down and— you don't know what going through their head, sometimes they want to run mad, sometimes they sit down, and they don't know what to do. Other than encouraging them, elders just watching at dem, like, look at how she ruins she life. Moreover, they don't know somebody came into

place and damage their child's life. And other than talk to the person, they just frown down on them and make them feel like, this is, this is not for me like I don't wanna live no more.

Participant 5: "First, you don't plan for it; it just happened, you know? Well, some people does plan for it, and some does come unexpectedly."

Participant 7:

I blame my mother for him (the child father) not looking after the child. Because she is always busing when he ain't bring anything and she gon' go and tell the man if he sure that is he child. I say, "Mommy, how would you do something like that? Because if you put me child father and me son together, they does look alike."

Participant 6: "Teach sex education in school, so it will help teenagers know the consequences if they get pregnant."

Participant 6:

What I'm thinking is whether what they can do when the individual is pregnant or before? They could introduce a prevention program so that persons would be aware of the stuff they should do or should not do. During the process, they should educate persons on their health, and the things that they should do after are providing prevention, which is the same thing as being cautious.

Summary

The findings reported in this chapter addressed the research questions of how social and economic consequences affect adolescent pregnancy. These findings have filled a gap in the literature of Guyana on adolescent pregnancy's social and economic consequences.

Data analysis identified the social, economic, and educational challenges adolescents experienced once they became pregnant and delivered. This chapter also identified unknowns through the following themes and codes: the reality of social norms; reflections about pregnancy; limited support from parents, participating men, or the baby's father; the effects of being a school dropout; the need for adolescent counseling; the need for reintegration; and adolescent mothers' sentiments about their plight and experiences during pregnancy and after delivery.

The next chapter is a culmination of discussions under the identified themes and subsets of the research question.

5. Discussion, Conclusions, Implications, and Recommendations

This chapter presents answers to the four research questions and information about the social and economic consequences of adolescent pregnancy.

The collection of data through different methods supported a rich narrative provided by the study participants, and analysis of the data led to the development of three codes that captured meaning in the data. The results of the study contain seven themes and subthemes:

1. The reality of social norms
2. Reflections about pregnancy—the adolescent's new role as a parent
3. Limited support from (a) parents, (b) participating men and adolescent boys, and (c) the church
4. The effects of dropping out of school—low earnings
5. Adolescent counseling—parents' responsibility
6. Reintegration—the way forward
7. Adolescents speaking out

The themes are based on a triangulation of the responses to the questionnaires, focus groups, and interviews. This chapter includes the transformation strategy I used to develop an educational program to be delivered via television and radio to create awareness of the effects of adolescent pregnancy.

The central objective of this qualitative study was to understand and identify the social and economic consequences an adolescent suffers when she becomes pregnant and after she delivers. This research has created a discussion that should attract the attention of the private sector, government, communities, and religious groups.

The answers to the research questions provide the necessary information that may have contributed to adolescent pregnancy, the social and economic consequences of the pregnancy, and an awareness of the motivating factors that may have contributed to the adolescent's decision to become pregnant. Additionally, the answers to the research question have created awareness of the problem of adolescent pregnancy.

This study did not set out to compare rates among ethnicities; however, it is of some significance that the findings identified a high percentage of adolescent pregnancy among Indo- and Afro-Guyanese girls. Notwithstanding, a previous study by UNICEF (2017) on the Indigenous women and children of Guyana confirmed that Amerindians in Regions 1, 7, 8, and 9 have the highest rates of adolescent pregnancy in the country, despite the actual population sizes within the 10 administrative regions of Guyana—the combined population of Regions 1, 7, 8, and 9 is smaller than that of any of the six administrative regions.

The information from this study should change the focus on pregnancy reduction from the current four regions to all 10 regions. Furthermore, the impact of adolescent pregnancy must be examined by a cross-section of subgroups—parents, families, the community, and governmental and nongovernmental agencies—to reduce its effects on the adolescent.

PAHO et al. (2017) reported that around the world, approximately 16 million girls aged 15–19 and 2 million girls younger than 15 years become pregnant each year. The study confirmed that Guyana has the second-highest rate of adolescent pregnancy in LAC.

The findings of this study have further confirmed the existence of social and economic consequences that occur in several settings. Unemployment, dropping out of school, some level of homelessness, resentment, and abandonment are consequences that seem to suggest that the future of adolescent mothers becomes imperiled as a result of pregnancy. Inadequate schooling and economic challenges suggest that adolescent pregnancy is not entirely a problem of the adolescent but is a feature of a system and a family that may have failed them. Literature dealing with the social and economic consequences of adolescent pregnancy is lacking although these consequences have a bearing on adolescent pregnancy. Moreover, previous studies on adolescent pregnancy in Guyana have not explicitly focused on the social and economic consequences of pregnancy and delivery.

While adolescent pregnancy is a well-known fact in Guyana, there are still gaps in perceptions about the factors that drive these pregnancies. My study confirmed that (a) adolescents' experiences with social and economic circumstances may have influenced their decision to become pregnant and (b) that the decisions of others complicate the adolescents' social and economic future in society.

5.1. Seven Themes or Reflections About Adolescent Pregnancy

5.1.1 Reality of Social Norms

This theme is in response to Q1: "What are the social circumstances adolescents face during pregnancy?" The existing literature emphasizes that adolescents are exposed to several socioeconomic factors and that these factors become compounded when pregnancy occurs. This list is "not limited to … the area of residence, parental, and social attitudes towards the adolescent mother," nor is it exhaustive (Paranjothy et al., 2009).

The challenges stated above no doubt affect social norms, and new family responsibilities force adolescents to end their schooling. The findings of this study suggest that participants strongly attribute poverty, parents' absence or lack of parental guidance, and lack of knowledge as some of the factors responsible for their predicament. The adolescents also experienced parental and societal resentment, which could have contributed to decisions that may have affected their future social and economic development. However, this resentment was not found in all cases of adolescent pregnancy because while there were similarities in some cases, there were differences grounded in individual settings. It can be concluded whatever the reason for the decisions adolescents make during the adolescent phase and even into young adulthood, these decisions can drastically change their futures if help is not given or sought. When one considers the critical elements that need to be addressed in terms of the adolescent's relational norms (peer pressure, expectations of family and peers, and support from the child's father), it becomes necessary for stakeholders to plot a development path to cope with these harsh elements.

Moreover, the focus group and interview findings of this study were reviewed, and the focus group participants provided more details concerning lived norms than did the interviewees. When parents or teachers discovered adolescent pregnancy, they often viewed it as a family shame, a shameful sin, or the end of the adolescent's future.

The need to terminate pregnancy becomes a priority because of anxiety, and the Abortion Act of 1995 makes termination lawful. Study participants revealed their plight when parents or guardians aggressively traumatized them into having an abortion as a family cover-up; however, the participants successfully resisted the temptation to have an abortion and could boast of either a future delivery date or a son or a daughter.

These reflections summarize the expressions that came from participants' responses to the research questions, which identified the gaps and untold truth concerning the social and economic challenges they experienced. Being a pregnant adolescent is a source of stigma. The perception of others of expectant adolescent mothers and the thoughts of others about these mothers' decisions can be challenging. The family structure sometimes prohibits adolescents from having a heart-to-heart conversation with their parents. Adolescents understand their reasons for dropping out of school or putting their education on hold. Evidence suggests that many adolescent mothers have yet to learn how to get out of the dilemma they find themselves in.

UNICEF (2016) pointed out that adolescent girls with no education or with only primary education are up to 4 times more likely to initiate childbearing compared with girls with secondary or higher education. Regarding psychosocial issues, adolescent pregnancy profoundly affects a girl's life trajectory and hampers her psychosocial development.

The findings of this study showed that adolescents seek conversations and love elsewhere, including from peers and anyone who will listen to their stories, regardless of their age. They are conscious of their current environment and desire a prosperous future.

Fielder and Carey (2010) reported that perceptions of peer pressure are significantly associated with dating attitudes and sexual activity. Moreover, the struggles of adolescents are evident in that they cannot adequately address the decisions they have taken.

The outcomes of adolescent pregnancy were the same whether or not the adolescent was emotionally overwhelmed or coerced to have sex. However, adolescents who have started having a conversation about their pregnancy have begun to find ways to survive, live, breathe, and make decisions for a bright future.

Tate and Copas (2010) pointed out that peer pressure can be viewed as the central mechanism of transmitting group norms and maintaining loyalties among group members. It can be negative or positive, unhelpful or valuable, and may influence teenagers to do things they would not normally do. Peer pressure can take on a life of its own and may persist because it is a phenomenon that enhances or frustrates the way of life of those under its influence.

The study's findings confirmed that many adolescents regretted the decision that led them to conceive. Furthermore, some claimed that their parents had neglected them before they became pregnant. Hence, when they became pregnant, they were finally forced to seek protection and accommodation from the state or enter into common law living, taking on roles that did not match their abilities. The findings also highlighted the many challenges such as discomfort, pain, and fear of death or complications that adolescents faced during pregnancy and after delivery.

5.1.2 New Roles as Parents

This theme is in response to Q2: "What are the behavioral circumstances adolescents experience after delivery?" An adolescent in the new role of a parent needs to accept training as a new parent. I found that 79.4% of adolescents agreed they needed mandatory classes to understand their roles as new parents. This decision should stimulate governmental and nongovernmental organizations to collaborate in developing a training plan. A comparison of survey findings indicates that most participants felt that reproductive health should be taught within the 14- to 18-year age range and not earlier. However, adolescent girls engage in sexual activities from as early as 11 years of age, which exposes them to early pregnancies (Hindin & Fatusi, 2009).

In the Guyanese context, there is evidence of early sexual activity, but once identified, the perpetrators are brought before court under the Sexual Offences Act. This study revealed that the ages of adolescents who become pregnant for whatever reason commenced at 11–14 years and peaked at 15 years. It is evident that if reproductive health is not addressed before age 14, then the dilemma and consequences of adolescent pregnancy will remain.

5.1.3 Limited Support

This theme is in response to Q3: "What are the economic challenges adolescents experience in the community?" This study found that adolescent mothers, whether pregnant or having delivered, have several regrets and wish to change their status in life. Everyone needs to be concerned with adolescent growth and development, educational attainment, and economic status. Furthermore, it is essential to give adolescents the necessary support to have a fulfilling future. A girl's decision to become pregnant, the involvement of the father in the pregnancy, and limited or no support from the father, the girl's parents, or the church can create long-term emotional and psychological stress.

5.1.3.1 Participating Fathers

In an earlier study conducted in Guyana, Rose et al. (2016) reported that 20% of the pregnant adolescents interviewed had partners who were at least 8 years older, and the most substantial age gap between the partners was as high as 32 years. The authors posited that "adolescent males are permanently absent or take on the role of a visiting non-supportive father or make a partial contribution that is grossly inadequate. In other settings, the adolescent male often cannot provide any support because he is unemployed" (p. 117).

This study identified a limited number of participating men—only nine (4% of the total participants). The low percentage of participating men is associated with the social and economic dilemmas that the adolescent mothers alluded to in the study. Also, the age gap between the female and male partner was 19–55 years, with the average age of the child's father being 24 years.

The child's father generally disappeared even before being told about the pregnancy. The visiting father, whose financial contributions cannot suffice to make ends meet, further adds to the economic challenges faced by the adolescent mother. The adolescent girl struggles to purchase clothing for her unborn child and even for herself, which often leads to seeking help from someone other than the child's father.

5.1.3.2 Parents

Participants reported being abandoned by their parents, being forced to leave the home where they grew up, and entering into common-law relationships. The mental and physical abuse contributed to additional poor decisions and maltreatment by partners. The study results also highlighted that adolescents' dreams were shattered and that they were lonely after being separated from their families by law and having the state take on the roles of protector and provider for them and their babies.

5.1.3.3 Roles of the Church

Based on my experience as an ordained minister, the church's role is to provide a space for love, kindness, and caring; looking out for all saints and those who are lost; providing spiritual food from the word of God; and giving supportive guidance. However, as with any other pregnancy out of wedlock, adolescent pregnancy is viewed by church members as a sin, and adolescents who become pregnant are relieved of their positions and tasks. Parents can prevent this shameful ordeal from occurring by voluntarily removing their child to a safe space. The results of this study confirm that some of the participants attended church regularly, while others attended occasionally.

Evidence from discussions with adolescents revealed that the church had not done much. Adolescents claimed that some members of the church ridiculed them. Further, adolescents exhibited signs of regret, and they were expected to improve after counseling and reintegration into a learning institution.

5.1.4 Effects of Dropping Out of School

In a study on adolescent pregnancy, Gomes (2012) noted that "without education or employable skills, pregnant adolescents [are] forced to drop out of school and are poorly prepared to take on the responsibilities of childrearing while facing diminished income prospects" (p. 133). Adolescent pregnancy has disrupted the future of many adolescents who were not resilient enough to recover from their shattered dreams and take a turn toward a promising future.

Paranjothy et al. (2009) argued that "pregnancy and childbirth during the adolescent years are associated with increased risk of poorer health and well-being for both the mother and the baby, possibly reflecting the socioeconomic factors that precede early pregnancy and childbirth." Hence, the effect on society is a perpetuation of the widening gap in health and social inequalities.

Furthermore, for young girls who live in deprived areas, pregnancy can increase the risk of social exclusion and socioeconomic disadvantage. Moreover, the adolescent understands the reason or reasons behind dropping out of school and putting her education on hold; however, she also realizes that she has the potential to turn her life around.

According to UNICEF (2019), several factors in Guyana contribute to adolescent pregnancy. These factors may not be recognized by law. The law regulates some cultural factors: the age of sexual consent and the age of marriage is age 16. For decades, the Indo-Guyanese gave parental consent to matched marriages of adolescent girls over age 13 to an older partner aged over 20. The cultural practice in Guyana where a son or daughter lives in a parent or parents' home after a licensed marriage, ceremonial marriage, or common-law relationship (unmarried persons living together as man and wife) is still practiced.

Adolescents are aware that their lack of education has contributed to their difficulty in securing employment, which forces them to take menial jobs or remain unemployed, thus increasing their financial problems. Adolescents also recalled their performance in school before being forced to leave school because of early pregnancy.

5.1.5 Need for Adolescent Counseling

PAHO and UNFPA (2020) reported that adolescent fertility rates were unacceptably high, with significant inequities between and within countries. They further reported that "girls from families in the lower wealth quintile, with lower levels of education, and from Indigenous and Afro-descendant communities are disproportionately affected by adolescent pregnancy" (p. 1).

The study participants expressed a desire to find a way out of their dilemma and viewed counseling as a primary source of transformation. The results highlighted the adolescents' confirmation of their negative attitudes toward their self-development and that they requested to be taught the themes of values and morals. Data from the study also revealed a need for some form of contraceptive or *a way to prevent pregnancy*.

The adolescents claimed they wanted someone to listen to them and not insult them as their parents and others had done. They wanted their parents to be responsible and caring and to accept them despite their situation. Adolescents need encouragement to help them improve and to influence them to make sound decisions in the future.

5.1.6 Reintegration is the Way Forward

This theme is in response to Q4: "What educational strategies should be developed and implemented to impact the psychosocial behaviors of adolescents?" The MOE (2018) established the National Policy for the Reintegration of Adolescent Mothers into the Formal Education System. This legislation assures the adolescent, whether pregnant or a mother, of her legal right to reregistration into the education system to complete her education. In this section, participants added to what their needs, described in the earlier paragraphs, were; however, the needs stated here are particularly strategic. The environment has influenced many adolescents negatively. There is also a class that, while not pregnant, experienced similar challenges of coercion, poverty, and the like that the pregnant adolescents and adolescent mothers experienced. Furthermore, there is another group of adolescents who become pregnant despite being aware of the difficulties experienced by their peers.

In this study, adolescents consistently asked for additional governmental intervention in the form of stiff penalties or court payments for child support. In the short term, the government could provide financial assistance so that the adolescents could be independent. The government could also set up training spaces only for pregnant adolescents and offer scholarships to adolescents as an incentive to complete their education.

5.1.7 Adolescents Speaking Out

It is astonishing how adolescents manipulate their parents and guardians by withholding important information to save themselves from embarrassment and protect perpetrators. The adolescents in this study were interested in having a sound relationship with their parents—a relationship of trust and understanding so that the truth could be told about incest, rape, coercion, and abuse and not what the adolescents thought their parents wanted to hear. Adolescents blame their parents for interfering in their relationships with their male partners.

Finally, being adolescent and pregnant may be stigmatized. Nevertheless, the truth is, "the trends of adolescent pregnancy rate in the Caribbean has [*sic*] singled out Guyana as having the highest rate: 91.1 per 1,000 girls [in the] 15–19 age range" (PAHO et al., 2017).

Evidence from this study seems to suggest that adolescents are either directly affected by or contribute to the dilemma of social and economic challenges as a result of poor decisions or lack of information. In a study regarding high-risk behaviors among adolescents in the Caribbean, Maharaj et al. (2009, p. 1) found that 19% of adolescents initiate sexual activity at around the age of 10 and that "adolescent pregnancy account [*sic*] for 15–20% of all pregnancies, and one-fifth of these adolescents were in their second pregnancy."

There is a program within the MOE Guyana called Health and Family Life Education. This program has been integrated into schools; its effectiveness has to be explored and evaluated via a prepared instrument.

5.2. Transformational Strategy to Implement CHANGE

The purpose of the proposed radio or television program is to bring awareness through an educational program developed from the results of this research. The findings suggest that adolescents are either directly affected by or contribute to social and economic dilemmas due to the adolescents' poor decisions or lack of information. Adolescent pregnancy is a challenge. The results of this study will be used to develop a relevant radio or television program to encourage adolescents to refrain from sexual activity and prevent pregnancy before they are ready for the resultant responsibility.

The high rates of adolescent pregnancy have not only affected the social and economic status of adolescents in the 10 administrative regions of Guyana but have also moved the nation to the second-highest place in the Caribbean and Latin America in terms of adolescent pregnancy rates. Evidence suggests that "the adolescent pregnancy rates for Guyana are at 91.1 per 1,000 girls" (PAHO et al., 2017), and these rates are highest in four of the 10 administrative regions of the country. The findings of this study confirmed that in Guyana, adolescent pregnancy is a problem that is coupled with the socioeconomic predicament of the adolescents who appear to have lost their way and have no future. Therefore, a transformational strategy is needed to change the mindset of adolescents to enable them to make informed decisions about the future.

I will use the lessons learned to structure the CHANGE program to address the core of the problem, which is the cultural adaptation of the societal norms that seem to influence the adolescent's decision to become pregnant. Based on the findings of this research project, I will deliver programming content in weekly broadcasts with the intent to institute a gradual change from societal beliefs.

It is my hope that as adolescents begin to understand the content of the CHANGE program, they will be motivated to move in the right direction, thus allowing them to be true to themselves while being influenced to make a difference in their society. Another goal of the program is to discourage adolescent girls from engaging in sexual activity so that they do not become pregnant. Moreover, for adolescent boys, the goal is to encourage them to be responsible and to delay their first sexual encounter to avoid impregnating girls. The broadcast programming will also focus on boys' personal development so they can become responsible men.

5.2.1 Appreciative Inquiry (AI)

To ensure excellent results, I adopted appreciative inquiry (AI) and the 4 Ds approach—discover, dream, design, and destiny—to forge a transformational process. This approach was used to stimulate adolescents to express themselves and to imagine themselves to be climbing to new levels while using the opportunity to design a way forward. I hope that adolescents will finally present themselves as transformed people ready to give back to society (Whitney & Trosten-Bloom, 2010).

5.2.2 Transformational Leadership

The eight transformational leadership perspectives of BGU (2021) are of considerable significance to the project, which aims to give hope and encourage trust, confidence, self-esteem, and a belief among adolescents that "I can do all things through him who gives me strength" (Philippians 4:13).

BGU's eight transformational perspectives are calling-based, incarnational, reflective, servant, contextual, global, shalom, and prophetic leadership. I will focus on two of BGU's transformational perspectives. These perspectives will undoubtedly provide an excellent framework for the type of transformation that will impact and foster resilience of the motherhood-in-childhood phenomenon among adolescents.

5.2.2.1 Calling-Based Leadership

According to the transformational leadership principles taught at BGU (2021), "the leader seeks to understand God-given gifts, experiences, and opportunities in understanding his/her unique role as a called instrument of Christ's transforming work in and above world cultures." In the context of this book, adolescents will be mentored and encouraged to understand that they are God's creation and born with God-given gifts. Moreover, the CHANGE program will aim to show adolescents that they need to use their gifts by making a meaningful contribution to society as they embrace new opportunities.

5.2.2.2 Incarnational Leadership

Incarnational leadership has been defined in the following way: "The leader pursues shared experiences, shared plights, shared hopes, in addition to shared knowledge and tasks" (BGU, 2021). I believe that as incarnational leaders who share the plight of others, we need to help adolescents understand what God promised through Jeremiah when He said to Israel, "I know the plans I have for you" (Jeremiah 29:11). In the context of this book, the incarnational leader is relevant since God has a plan irrespective of the adolescent's deviation. According to BGU (2016), an incarnational leader is one who is always present to feel others' plight. The incarnational leader will share relevant experiences to motivate and encourage adolescents to rethink their positions. Additionally, the leader will highlight the issues to be addressed and work with the adolescent until she understands and values herself. Incarnational leaders also need to facilitate adolescent participation in community work so that the adolescent can be included in the conversation, which is necessary in embracing God's plan for community transformation.

Local arrangements will be put in place to convince governmental and nongovernmental institutions of interest to develop or implement existing programs that will attract attention and create resilience among adolescents. These programs will be designed to create an atmosphere that reduces sexual encounters. Hopefully, as a community, we will be able to (a) explore the drivers of the decisions adolescents make that change their future, (b) explore the adolescents' understanding of issues and challenges, and (c) help the adolescents who become mothers to plot a way back to acceptable standards that will allow them to make progress in life.

As a televangelist, public health professional, and teacher, I can positively influence teenagers in Guyana. The proposed broadcast programming will provide a second chance for adolescents in the country. The incarnational leadership perspective will undoubtedly afford an excellent framework for the type of transformation that will impact and foster the resilience of the motherhood-in-childhood phenomenon among adolescents in the nation.

I plan to devise means to bring about new ways of thinking using the acronym CHANGE (challenge, holistic, awareness, negotiate, generate interest, and esteem). This goal will be accomplished through a nationwide initiative to be implemented through a nonprofit organization called CHANGE. Making good on my promise to implement this initiative upon completion of my doctoral studies, I am elated to announce that it will come into effect mid-2023. This organization will collaborate with other stakeholders to disseminate information on adolescent best practices and challenges via national television and national radio of Guyana, which are aired across the 10 regions of Guyana.

5.2.3 Program Objectives

In light of the findings that confirmed that there are social and economic challenges that result from adolescent pregnancy, I identified program objectives to be critical factors that will give direction to the specific and urgent gap that needs to be filled for transformational processes to be accepted.

The objectives of the CHANGE program are as follows:

1. Discuss the benefits of delaying sexual debut.
2. Discuss the social and economic setbacks that occur when an adolescent becomes pregnant.
3. Reinforce messaging about the need for educational attainment and how it affects job recruitment.

5.2.4 Action Plan

Transformational intervention aims to bring shalom to both adolescents and parents or guardians, and the project implementation will create awareness to address the problem of adolescent pregnancy through radio, television, and seminars and at the community level. I will identify and adopt best practices and programs that have led to the reduction of adolescent pregnancy in other contexts. Focus will also be on delivery issues, lactating mothers, health challenges during labor and delivery, financial and accommodation challenges, acceptance by the father, and rejection by family.

These issues are specific to the events that will occur during and after delivery and reflect the readiness of the adolescent's physical development to accommodate such changes. From the gynecological perspective, labor and delivery are not always without incident. Sometimes it takes major or minor surgery to birth the baby vaginally or abdominally because of cephalopelvic disproportion. Also, according to the findings, there is a need for training to encourage the participating man and the adolescent's parents to be responsible and supportive of the adolescent mother and her child. The participating man will be urged to be financially supportive to help alleviate the dilemmas faced by the adolescent mother.

5.2.5 Transformational Methodology

I will use the *Ebenezer Praise Time* program televised on National Communications Network channel 11 to disseminate information weekly. Furthermore, I will employ *Voice of Guyana Radio* that airs on National Communications Network, 98.1 FM to share content fortnightly. My content will address issues such as the social and economic challenges that arise due to adolescent pregnancy and the need for an adolescent to make educational attainments. Moreover, adolescent mothers will be invited to share their experiences publicly through seminars and coaching sessions to develop an approach grounded on CHANGE. I will regularly evaluate the program to determine the impact of the understanding of adolescent pregnancy, the adolescent's educational attainment, and changes in socioeconomic status.

5.2.6 Program Content

As noted previously, the program will be developed based on research findings; therefore, the program topics will be developed to fill the gaps identified in the study's results. The topic contents will include the following areas:

1. Defining sexuality
2. Defining an adolescent
3. Defining adolescent pregnancy
4. Growth and development between 0–19 years
    - (a) infancy, (b) preschool, (c) puberty, and (d) adolescence

5. Menstruation
6. Defining the adolescent age of consent in Guyana
7. Resisting peer pressure
8. Benefits of abstinence
9. Second chances
10. Social implications of adolescent pregnancy
    - effects of homelessness
11. Economic implications of adolescent pregnancy
    - (a) absence of a male participant and (b) nonsupport from parents/guardians
12. Educational implication of adolescent pregnancy
    - dropping out of school
13. Benefit of reintegration in educational institutions
14. Development of coping skills

Regarding the audience for this program, the National Television Network has 90% coverage throughout Guyana and is the best way of disseminating information to a critical mass.

5.2.7 Evaluation

I plan to develop an instrument to measure the radio and television program's success and identify the gaps, if any, in program delivery and level of awareness. According to Mkandawire (2010), "Evaluation is the process of examining a program or process to determine what is working, what is not, and why. It determines the value of learning and training programs and acts as blueprints [*sic*] for judgment and improvement."

With these objectives in mind, the questionnaire developed was designed to obtain in-depth information from a cross-section of people, particularly adolescent boys and girls, including those who are currently pregnant or are adolescent mothers. The questionnaire responses will confirm the level of awareness and its potential to create the fundamental change that is expressed outwardly in the adolescent's new life. Another method of obtaining immediate feedback from viewers will be through a five-minute call-in segment during the weekly television and biweekly radio programs.

5.3 Recommendations

5.3.1 Government Ministries and NGOs

This study confirmed that the rate of adolescent pregnancy in Guyana is the second highest in LAC. Over the last 5 years, the government has begun to take action through selected ministries such as the Ministries of Education and Health and other stakeholders. The development of programs will mainly be done in Region 4 to help the adolescent deal with pregnancy and delivery and afford her the capacity to cope after delivery. However, the effectiveness of the programs has yet to be measured. While there is a need for further establishment of similar programs in other regions, I make the following recommendations with this need in mind:

1. The MOE should reinforce or implement and sustain the Health and Family Life Education program for all children within the school-age range.

2. The MOE should reinforce awareness about the reintegration and reregistration program for adolescent mothers in all 10 administrative regions.

3. The MOE should recruit additional counselors and establish a counseling unit in all primary, secondary, and skills-based schools.

4. The MOPH, in collaboration with the MOE, should establish parenting classes for all adolescent mothers in all administrative regions.

5. Relevant organizations should be encouraged to establish a stakeholder evaluation of their specific programs' effectiveness and the adolescent outcomes of program completion.

6. In collaboration with the MOE, churches and other religious organizations should establish programs that will facilitate transition to adolescence.

7. The Government of Guyana, in collaboration with NGOs, should establish additional adolescent-friendly spaces so adolescent mothers can be encouraged to share their stories.

    a. Skills-based training centers should be established in all administrative regions as a part of the reintegration mechanism.

b. Relevant policies should be established in keeping with adolescent safety and job opportunities while all existing policies for adolescents should be legislated and enforced.

5.4 Recommendations for Further Research

This research has underscored that Guyana indeed has an adolescent pregnancy issue that may worsen the plight of adolescents and their helplessness in coping with the stressors in society and the economic challenges they face during pregnancy and delivery. A significant outcome of my project will be the implementation of a program developed for radio and television to educate adolescents to engage in informed decision-making. This project will also give the adolescents some public awareness and support, which is integral to sustaining the adolescents' decisions.

I will, therefore, recommend further research into the following areas to increase understanding of the negative responses identified in the study by adolescents about parenting and to address the paucity of information concerning the involvement of men in adolescent pregnancies: (a) knowledge, attitude, and practice of parenting in the Guyanese setting and (b) understanding the meaning of fatherhood and fathering children, responsibilities, and new roles of fathers.

Final Thoughts

This qualitative study explored the social and economic consequences of adolescent pregnancy in the Guyanese context. The results of the study will be used to develop a program that will raise awareness of the consequences of adolescent pregnancy. The study focused on the social, economic, and educational situation of adolescents who are either pregnant or have delivered a child within the last 3 years. The findings fostered an initiative to develop a program that will raise awareness of adolescent pregnancy through weekly radio and television programming. The findings of the study also highlighted truths about the social and economic consequences of pregnancy for adolescents in Guyana.

Chapter 1 provided an introduction to the problem, purpose, research questions, and health and economic implications of adolescent pregnancy. A conceptual framework that established the boundaries for the research and guided the literature review was also described.

Chapter 2, the literature review, included prior and current information on social, economic, educational, and spiritual factors that have a bearing on adolescent pregnancy. This chapter also exposed gaps in knowledge about the social and economic consequences of adolescent pregnancy.

In Chapter 3, the methodology, study design, and framework for data collection and analysis were established. Descriptions of the field population, stakeholders, and instruments were provided, as well as the steps taken to collect and measure data. Selecting data from multiple sources allowed for the combination of the findings of this study and findings described in the literature.

Chapter 4 presented data collected from the field study and the results and findings of the data analysis. The data analysis resulted in the development of seven themes derived from data related to the social and economic consequences of adolescent pregnancy:

1. The reality of social norms
2. Reflections about pregnancy—the adolescents' new roles as parents
3. Limited support from parents, participating men, and the church
4. Effects of dropping out of school—low earnings
5. Adolescent counseling—parents' responsibility
6. Reintegration—the way forward
7. Adolescents speaking out

Chapter 5 included discussions, implications, and conclusions of discussions about the social and economic consequences of adolescent pregnancy. The discussions were based on the research questions and supporting themes and subthemes.

The text from the data collection instruments, as reproduced in Chapter 4, highlighted direct quotes from adolescents. The adolescents expressed regret for the decisions they made based on inadequate knowledge about what they were doing. The adolescents reported experiences with resentment from their parents, community, and church. They hoped to be counseled and given a second chance to realize their full potential and advocated for both financial and skills training interventions from governmental and nongovernmental organizations. The government's reintegration program is a public policy that gives the adolescent access to reregistration in school after she delivers. The policy also facilitates skills-based training through the MOE and WAD.

Chapter 5 also presented a program that was developed from the findings of this study. This program will be used to spread awareness about adolescent pregnancy through radio and television programs, workshops, and seminars.

References

Ali, S., Mohammed, S., & Mungrue, K. (2009). The epidemiology of unplanned pregnancies in North-Central Trinidad. *International Journal of Adolescent Medicine and Health*, *21*(1), 73–78. https://doi.org/10.1515/IJAMH.2009.21.1.73

Ahamad, R. (2017, March 7). Underage marriages a worrying scenario. *Kaieteur News*. https://www.kaieteurnewsonline.com/2017/03/07/underage-marriages-a-worrying-scenario/

Arceo-Gómez, E. O., & Campos-Vázquez, R. M. (2014). Teenage pregnancy in Mexico: Evolution and consequences. *Latin American Journal of Economics*, *51*(1), 109–146. http://dx.doi.org/10.7764/LAJE.51.1.109

ATLAS.ti 8 Windows. (2019). User manual updated for program version 8.4. Qualitative data analysis. https://atlasti.cleverbridge.com/74/?=cart&cart=13731&x-ident=HOLDER-071808019-0

Azevedo, J. P., Favara, M., Haddock, S. E., Lopez-Calva, L. F., Muller, M., & Perova, E. (2012). *Teenage pregnancy and opportunities in Latin America and the Caribbean on early childbearing, poverty, and economic achievement (Vol. 2): Teenage pregnancy book 2013* (English). World Bank Group. http://documents.worldbank.org/curated/en/638771468017359353/Teenage- pregnancy-book-2013

Bakke Graduate University. (2021). *Transformational leadership perspectives*. https://bgu.edu/transformational-leadership-perspectives

Bliss, L. B. (2008). Media review: Greene, J. C. (2007). Mixed methods in social inquiry. *Journal of Mixed Methods Research*, 2(2). https://doi.org/10.1177/1558689807314013

Breen, R. L. (2007). A practical guide to focus-group research. *Journal of Geography in Higher Education*, *30*(3), 463–475. https://doi.org/10.1080/03098260600927575

Bulkan, J. (2013). The struggle for recognition of the Indigenous voice: Amerindians in Guyanese politics. *The Round Table*, *102*(4), 367–380. https://doi.org/10.1080/00358533.2013.795009

Bureau of Statistics. (2018). *Guyana multiple indicator cluster survey*. https://statisticsguyana.gov.gy/surveys/

Bureau of Statistics, Ministry of Public Health, and United Nations Children's Fund. (2015). *Guyana: Multiple indicator cluster survey 2014*. BoS, MOPH, & UNICEF. https://www.unicef.org/guyanasuriname/media/611/file/MICS-5-2014-Report.pdf

Burns, J. M. (1998). *Leadership*. Harper & Row.

Carlson, M. J., & McLanahan, S. S. (2004). Early father involvement in fragile families. In R. D. Day & M. E. Lamb (Eds.), *Conceptualizing and measuring father involvement* (pp. 241–271). Lawrence Erlbaum Associates. https://core.ac.uk/download/pdf/6258052.pdf

Chandra-Mouli, V., Camacho, A. V., & Michaud, P. A. (2013). *WHO guidelines on preventing early pregnancy and poor reproductive outcomes among adolescents in developing countries.* WHO. https://doi.org/10.1016/j.jadohealth.2013.03.002

Constitution of the Cooperative Republic of Guyana Act. (1980). https://www.oas.org/juridico/spanish/mesicic2_guy_constitution.pdf

Corbett, S., & Fikkert, B., (2014). *When helping hurts: How to alleviate poverty without hurting the poor... and yourself.* Moody.

Creswell, J. W., & Creswell, J. D. (2017). *Research design: Qualitative, quantitative, and mixed methods approach.* Sage.

Creswell, J. W., & Plano C. V. (2017). *Designing and conducting mixed methods research*: Sage.

Daly, V. T. (1974). *The making of Guyana.* MacMillan Publishing Company.

Fielder, R. L., & Carey, M. P. (2010). Predictors and consequences of sexual "hookups" among college students: A short-term prospective study. *Archives of Sexual Behavior, 39*(5), 1105–1119. https://doi.org/10.1007/s10508-008-9448-4

Finkelhor, D. (1984). *Child sexual abuse.* Free Press.

Ganchimeg, T., Ota, E., Morisaki, N., Laopaiboon, M., Lumbiganon, P., Zhang, J., Yamdamsuren, B., Temmerman, M., Say, L., Tunçalp, Ö., Vogel, J. P., Souza, J. P., & Mori, R. (2014). Pregnancy and childbirth outcomes among adolescent mothers: A World Health Organization multicountry study. *British Journal of Obstetrics and Gynaecology*, *121*(suppl. 1), 40–48. https://doi.org/10.1111/1471-0528.12630

Gill, P., Stewart, K., Treasure, E., & Chadwick, B. (2008). Methods of data collection in qualitative research: Interviews and focus groups. *British Dental Journal*, *204*(6), 291–295. https://doi.org/10.1038/bdj.2008.192

Gomes, C. (2012). Adolescent fertility in selected countries of Latin America and the Caribbean. *Journal of Public Health and Epidemiology*, *4*(5), 133–140. https://doi.org/10.5897/JPHE11.208

Goodman, M., & Dollahite, D. (2006). How religious couples perceive the influence of God in their marriage. *Review of Religious Research*, *48*(2), 141–155. www.jstor.org/stable/20058129

Greene, J. C., Caracelli, J., & Graham, W. F. (1989). Toward a conceptual framework for mixed-method evaluation designs. *Educational Evaluation and Policy Analysis*, *11*(3), 225–274. https://www.jstor.org/stable/1163620

Gulati, S. (2017). Impact of peer pressure on buying behavior. *International Journal of Research-Granthaalayah*, *5*(6). https://doi.org/10.5281/zenodo.820988

Guyana Chronicle. (2014, May 27). *First peoples of Guyana.* https://guyanachronicle.com/2014/05/27/first-peoples-of-guyana/

Guyana News and Information. (n.d.) *Synopsis of Guyana.* http://www.guyananews.org/guymap.html

Haglund, K., & Fehring, R. (2010). The association of religiosity, sexual education, and parental factors with risky sexual behaviors among adolescents and young adults. *Journal of Religion and Health, 49*(4), 460–472. www.jstor.org/stable/40961600

Hall, B., & Howard, K. (2008). A synergistic approach: Conducting mixed methods research with typological and systemic design considerations. *Journal of Mixed Methods Research, 2*(3). https://doi.org/10.1177/1558689808314622

Hamilton, L. (2017, November 11). Spotlight on teenage pregnancy in outlying areas. *Guyana Chronicle.* https://guyanachronicle.com/2017/11/11/spotlight-on-teenage-pregnancy-in-outlying-areas/

Hindin, M. J., & Fatusi, A. O. (2009). Adolescent sexual and reproductive health in developing countries: An overview of trends and interventions. *International Perspectives on Sexual and Reproductive Health, 35*(2), 58–62. http://dx.doi.org/10.1363/ipsrh.35.058.09

History of Guyana. (2023, March 17). In *Wikipedia.* https://en.wikipedia.org/wiki/History_of_Guyana#Precolonial_Guyana_and_first_contacts

International Centre for Research on Women (2018). *The economic impacts of child marriage: Key findings.* World Bank. https://www.icrw.org/wp-content/uploads/2018/07/EICM-GlobalSynthesisSummary_Report_v3_WebReady.pdf

Jennings, Z. (1999). Educational reform in Guyana in the post-war period. In E. Miller (Ed.), *Education reform in the Commonwealth Caribbean.* Organization of American States. http://www.educoas.org/Portal/bdigital/contenido/interamer/BkIACD/Interamer/Interamerhtml/Millerhtml/mil_jen.htm

Jeynes, W. H. (2009). *A call for character education and prayer in the schools.* Praeger.

Lalor, K. M., & McElvaney, R. (2010). Child sexual abuse links to later sexual exploitation/high-risk sexual behavior and prevention/treatment programs. *Trauma, Violence, Abuse, 11*(4), 159–177. https://doi.org/10.1177/1524838010378299

Loaiza, E., & Liang, M. (2013). Adolescent pregnancy: A review of the evidence. UNFPA. https://www.unfpa.org/publications/adolescent-pregnancy

Lopoo, L. M. (2011). Labor and delivery complications among teenage mothers. *Biodemography Social Biology, 57*(2), 200–220. https://doi.org/10.1080/19485565.2011.614915

Lund, C., Breen, A., Flisher, A. J., Kakuma R., Corrigall, J., Joska, J. A., Swartz, L., & Patel, V. (2010). Poverty and common mental disorders in low- and middle-income countries: A systematic review. *Social Science & Medicine*, *71*(3), 517–28. https://doi.org/10.1016/j.socscimed.2010.04.027

Maharaj, R. G., Nunes, P., & Renwick, S. (2009). Health risk behaviours among adolescents in the English-speaking Caribbean: A review. *Child and Adolescent Psychiatry and Mental Health*, *3*(1), 10. https://www.doi:10.1186/1753-2000-3-10

McCaw-Binns, A., Bailey, A., Holder-Nevins, D., & Alexander, S., (2012). Adverse consequences of uninformed adolescent sex in Jamaica: From STIs to pregnancy, abortion, and maternal death. *Social and Economic Studies, (61)*3, 145–166. https://www.jstor.org/stable/41803771

McLeish, J., & Redshaw, M. (2015). Peer support during pregnancy and early parenthood: A qualitative study of models and perceptions. *BMC Pregnancy Childbirth*, *15*, 257. https://doi.org/10.1186/s12884-015-0685-y

Ministry of Education. (2011). Health and family life education: Grade 1 through 9 curriculum guides [Guyana]. https://education.gov.gy/en/

Ministry of Education. (2018). *National policy: Reintegration of adolescent mothers into the formal school system, with technical and financial support from the United Nations Children Fund (UNICEF)*. UNICEF. https://www.unicef.org/guyanasuriname/media/471/file/National-Policy-Reintegration-of-Adolescent_Mothers_into-Formal_School-System.pdf

Ministry of Public Health, Adolescent Health Unit. (2018). *Manual: Accelerated Action for the Health of Adolescents (AA-HA!). Situational analysis of adolescents health in Guyana.* Collaboration with PAHO/WHO, UNFPA, UNICEF. Ministry of Public Health, Guyana.

Mistry, J., Berardi, A., Tschirhart, C., Bignante, E., Haynes, L., Benjamin, R., & De Ville, G. (2015). Indigenous identity and environmental governance in Guyana, South America. *Cultural Geographies, 22*(4), 689–712. www.jstor.org/stable/26168684

Merriam, S. B., & Tisdell, E. J. (2016). *Qualitative research: A guide to design and implementation.* Jossey-Bass.

Mkandawire, S. B. (2010). Role of formative and summative evaluation in curriculum development [Blog post]. https://sitwe.wordpress.com/2010/10/29/the-role-of-formative-and-summative-and-summative-evaluation-in-curriculum-development/

Moldes, V. M., Biton, C. L., Gonzaga, D. J., & Moneva, J. C. (2019). Students, peer pressure and their academic performance in school. *International Journal of Scientific and Research Publications, 9*(1), 300–312. http://dx.doi.org/10.29322/IJSRP.9.01.2019.p8541

Pan American Health Organization & United Nations Population Fund. (2020). *Adolescent pregnancy in Latin America and the Caribbean. Technical Brief.* https://lac.unfpa.org/sites/default/files/pub-pdf/final_dec_10_approved_policy_brief_design_ch_adolescent.pdf

Pan American Health Organization, United Nations Population Fund, & United Nations Children's Fund. (2017). *Accelerating progress toward the reduction of adolescent pregnancy in Latin America and the Caribbean. Report of a Technical Consultation: August 29–30, 2016; Washington, DC, USA.* https://lac.unfpa.org/sites/default/files/pub-pdf/Accelerating%20progress%20toward%20the%20reduction%20of%20adolescent%20pregnancy%20in%20LAC%20-%20FINAL.pdf

Paranjothy, S., Broughton, H., Adappa, R., & Fone, D. (2009). Teenage pregnancy: Who suffers? *Archives of Disease in Childhood, 94*(3), 239–245. http://dx.doi.org/10.1136/adc.2007.115915

Parker, W. C. (2006). Deploying Foucault: Purposes and Consequences. *Counterpoints, 272,* 237–240. http://www.jstor.org/stable/42978912

Parsons, C. E., Young, K. S., Rochat, T. J., Kringelbach, M., & Stein, A. (2012). Postnatal depression and its effects on child development: A review of evidence from low- and middle-income countries. *British Medical Bulletin, 101*(1). https://doi.org/10.1093/bmb/ldr047

Phipps-Yonas, S. (1980). Teenage pregnancy and motherhood: A review of the literature. *American Journal of Orthopsychiatry, 50*(3), 403–431.

Piazza, J. (2012). "If you love me, keep my commandments": Religiosity increases performance for rule-based moral arguments. *International Journal for the Psychology of Religion, 22*(4), 285–302. https://doi.org/10.1080/10508619.2011.638598

Rose, E. M., Rajasingam, D., Derkenne, R. C., Mitchell, V., & Ramlall, A. A. (2016). Reproductive health knowledge, attitudes, and practices of adolescents attending an obstetric unit in Georgetown, Guyana. *Journal of Family Planning & Reproductive Health Care, 42*(2), 116–118.

Schalet, A. T., Santelli, J. S., Russell, S. T., Halpern, C. T., Miller, S. A., Pickering, S. S. & Hoenig, J. M. (2014). Invited commentary: Broadening the evidence for adolescent sexual and reproductive health and education in the United States. *Journal of Youth and Adolescence, 43*, 1595–1610. https://doi.org/10.1007/s10964-014-0178-8

Senderowitz, J. (1995). *Adolescent health: Reassessing the passage to adulthood.* World Bank discussion papers, no. WDP 272. World Bank Group. http://documents.worldbank.org/curated/en/278081468739243027/Adolescent-health-reassessing-the-passage-to-adulthood

Sensing, T. (2011). *Qualitative research: A multi-methods approach to projects for doctor of ministry theses.* Wipf and Stock.

Sisson, G. (2012). Finding a way to offer something more: Reframing teen pregnancy prevention. *Sexuality Research Social Policy, 9*(1), 57–69. http://dx.doi.org/10.1007/s13178-011-0050-5

Stabroek News. (2012, July 13). *Common-law unions inheritance bill passed.* https://www.stabroeknews.com/2012/07/13/news/guyana/common-law-unions-inheritance-bill-passed/

Tashakkori, A., & Teddlie, C. B. (1998). *Mixed methodology: Combining qualitative and quantitative approaches.* Sage.

Tate, T. F., & Copas, R. L. (2010). "Peer pressure" and the group process: Building cultures of concern. *Reclaiming Children and Youth, 19*(1), 12–16.

Tebb, K. P., & Brindis, C. D. (2020). Understanding the psychological impacts of teenage pregnancy through a socio-ecological framework and life course approach. Seminars in Reproductive Medicine, 40(1–02), 107–115. http://doi.org/10.1055/s-0041-1741518.

Thomas, G. (2015). *Sacred marriage* [eBook edition]. Zondervan.

Torche, F. (2010). Change and persistence of intergenerational mobility in Mexico. In J. Serrano & F. Torche (Eds.), *Social mobility in Mexico. Population, development, and growth* (pp. 71–134). Espinosa Yglesias Study Center.

United Nations Children's Fund (2009). *The state of the world's children 2010: Special edition. Celebrating 20 years of the Convention on the Rights of the Child.* UNICEF. https://www.unicef.org/reports/state-worlds-children-2010

United Nations Children's Fund (2016). Guyana: Situation analysis of children and women. UNICEF. https://www.unicef.org/guyanasuriname/media/481/file/SitAn-Report-Teenage-Pregnacy.pdf

United Nations Children's Fund (2017). *Report. Study on Indigenous women and children in Guyana.* UNICEF. https://www.unicef.org/lac/en/reports/study-indigenous-women-and-children-guyana

United Nations Children's Fund. (2019). A profile of child marriage and early unions in Latin America and the Caribbean. UNICEF. https://www.unicef.org/lac/media/8256/file/Profile%20of%20Child%20Marriage%20in%20LAC.pdf

United Nations Population Fund. (2010) Sexual and reproductive health for all reducing poverty, advancing development, and protecting human rights. https://www.unfpa.org/publications/sexual-and-reproductive-health-all

Walker, S. P., Wachs, T. D., Gardner J. M., Lozoff, B., Wasserman, G. A., Pollitt, E., & Carter, J. A. (2007). Child development: Risk factors for adverse outcomes in developing countries. *The Lancet, 369*(9556),145–57.

Whitney, D. D., & Trosten-Bloom, A. (2010). *The power of appreciative inquiry: A practical guide to positive change.* Berrett-Koehler.

Yazdkhasti, M., Pourreza, A., Pirak, A., & Abdi, F. (2015). Unintended pregnancy and its adverse social and economic consequences on health system: A narrative review article. *Iranian Journal of Public Health, 44*(1), 12–21. http://ijph.tums.ac.ir/index.php/ijph/issue/view/480

Appendix A: Questionnaire

Adolescent Pregnancy Questionnaire Sheet (adapted from Survey Monkey)

Please tick (√) and/or insert all answers applicable to you for questions 1–17.

1. Current age____

    Pregnant ☐ Mother ☐ Male Participant ☐ Parent ☐

    Region: _____

    Race/Ethnicity: African ☐ East Indian ☐ Chinese ☐ Portuguese ☐ European ☐ Amerindian ☐ Mixed ☐

2. At what age should an adolescent be educated on pregnancy? ____

3. Should birth control or condoms be offered to underage persons?

    Yes ☐ No ☐

4. Should we offer counseling to adolescents who are pregnant?

    Yes ☐ No ☐

5. Should abortion options be given to adolescents without the consent of parents?

    Yes ☐ No ☐

6. Should there be a limit on how many abortions a woman can have?

    Yes ☐ No ☐

The LAWS OF GUYANA SEXUAL OFFENCES ACT CHAPTER 8:03 – (3): A person who commits an offense under subsection (1) is liable, on summary conviction, to imprisonment for five years and on conviction on indictment, to imprisonment for ten years.

7. Should there be stricter statutory rape laws in Guyana?

    Yes ☐   No ☐

8. Should children under the age of 16 be forced to have an abortion?

    Yes ☐   No ☐

9. Should classes be mandated for new parents?

    Yes ☐   No ☐

10. Should parents be held responsible for their children having children at a young age?

    Yes ☐   No ☐

11. How old were you the first time you were pregnant?

    _____

12. How old was the person who got you pregnant?

    _____

13. Why did you become pregnant as a teenager?

    ☐ I expected my partner to use contraception.

    ☐ I had no access to contraception (including the morning-after pill).

    ☐ I thought I could not get pregnant.

☐ Contraceptive failure.

☐ I was/felt pressured into having unprotected sex.

☐ I wanted to show I loved my partner.

☐ I got caught up in the moment.

☐ I was in an unstable relationship but wanted to start a family.

☐ I was embarrassed/it felt awkward to ask my partner to use a contraceptive.

☐ I did not feel comfortable obtaining contraception (including the morning-after pill).

☐ I was drunk and did not think.

☐ I was in a stable relationship and wanted to start a family.

☐ I was not too bothered about getting pregnant.

14. What were your reasons for deciding to continue with the pregnancy?

☐ I did not agree with getting an abortion.

☐ I did not feel I could go through with an abortion/I did not think about options.

☐ I did not know about other options.

☐ I felt pressured not to have an abortion.

☐ I did not feel I had a choice.

☐ I wanted a baby/It was planned. I thought I could be a good mum.

☐ I thought it must have happened for a reason.

☐ I wanted a baby.

☐ I felt that I should take responsibility.

☐ I wanted my partner to stay with me.

☐ I knew I had support from my family/partner.

15. Do you think those having sex with an underage person should be prosecuted?

   ☐ Always

   ☐ If force is used

   ☐ If the person under 16 reports it

   ☐ If the other person is aged 16–17

   ☐ If the other person is aged 18–24

   ☐ If the other person is aged 25–29

   ☐ If the other person is 30 or over

   ☐ If the person under 16 is considered vulnerable

16. What would you suggest should be done to reduce the rates of unplanned adolescent pregnancies?

   ☐ Provide improved access to/increase availability of contraception

   ☐ Provide more young people–friendly services

   ☐ Provide improved sex and relationship education in schools

- ☐ Provide improved support/advice for parents to talk to their teens
- ☐ Improve the aspirations of young people generally
- ☐ Focus on the responsibility of boys and men
- ☐ Strengthen the Child Care and Protection Agency
- ☐ Increase protection from abuse
- ☐ Increase stigma around teenage parenthood

17. Guyana has the highest rates of adolescent pregnancy in Latin America and the Caribbean. Why do you think this might be?

....

....

....

....

Appendix B: Focus Group and One-On-One Interview Questions

The questions below will be used in all the focus group sessions.

Exploration

a. How do you respond to an adolescent who is pregnant?

b. How do people respond to an adolescent who is pregnant?

Engagement

c. What are factors that contribute to the struggles of an adolescent mother to make ends meet?

d. What are the social circumstances adolescents experience during pregnancy?

e. What are the behavioral circumstances adolescents experience after delivery?

f. What are the economic challenges a pregnant adolescent experiences in the community?

g. What are the economic challenges a pregnant adolescent may experience at home?

h. What can parents do to allow pregnant adolescents to experience a prosperous future?

i. What can the government do to allow pregnant adolescents to experience a prosperous future?

j. What can the church and other religious institutions do to mitigate the economic consequences of adolescent pregnancy?

Exit Question

k. What final words do you have on adolescent pregnancy?

Made in the USA
Columbia, SC
18 January 2024